MW01518202

REIKI FOR BEGINNERS

Your Guide to Reiki Healing and Reiki Meditation With Useful Techniques to Increase Your Energy and Cleansing your Aura

EMILY ODDO

CONTENTS

INTRODUCTION

"If you want to find the secrets of the universe, think in terms of energy, frequency, and vibration." – Nikola Tesla

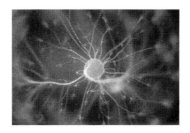

Imagine for a moment that you are exhausted. You have just had a long day following a night of little sleep because you had to work late into the evening. In the next five minutes, a meeting will start. You do not have enough energy to walk to the boardroom, let alone concentrate on the content of the meeting or maintain an appearance of vivacity. What do you do? There is no way you could get out of the meeting. Perhaps you could get coffee, but you have lost count of the number of coffees you have already had, and after each cup, you feel more feeble —more drained.

Perhaps instead you could just grab a cup of water. Yet, sincerely, you do not even have the strength for that. You need something that can get you out of your seat first. So, what do you do? Your face collapses into the palms of your hands. You breathe deeply as they are cupping your face. If you press deeply into your palms, it's possible the blood vessels in your eyes will make an imprint into your fingers, making you feel as if you are looking at a galaxy. It is just your blood vessels, but this impression seems outer-worldly.

For two minutes, you continue in this state, lying with your head cupped in your palms, breathing in your hands, and watching the galaxy continually shapeshift. Before the five minutes elapses, you are on your feet walking downstairs to the boardroom, not perfect, but not completely defeated, either. Some revival has occurred. If you are conscious enough, you make a mental note to take a quick headrest during the meeting—if you can get away with it.

This headrest forms the basics of how Reiki works (Reiki Self-Treatment: Procedure Details, 2019). Though you may have taken breaks cupping your face in your hands in the past, you may have not realized that what you were doing was a Reiki hand position. As your hands support your face, you feel the warmth and energy from them. The hands are channels of energy. Thus, when you relax your face into them, the energy between your face and hands flow. This leaves you feeling relaxed and revitalized.

Moreover, this collapse of your head into your hands is an unconscious reaction. You do not decide to rest your face into your hands, but as your lack of energy plummets, you give in and let your head fall. Five minutes later, you feel better and more prepared to go about your day. In this sense, Reiki is an unconscious, primordial form of healing. As a reflex, you rely on it when all other reserves have failed.

If two minutes of Reiki can give you enough energy to overcome debilitating exhaustion, can you imagine what half an hour each day could do?

THE CRISIS IN ENERGY

In the contemporary world, we have a crisis in energy. The recent rise in the number of burnout cases and unprecedented levels of stress and anxiety show that modern people are severely lacking energy (Elflein, 2016). The insane levels of competition to obtain skills and well-paying jobs does not do anything to help rejuvenate people. However, while there is a general consensus that stress and burnout is a major present-day problem, not everyone agrees on the roots of this issue.

Yet, what is burnout other than a crisis in energy? The clue is in the name. Even the word stress suggests the fundamental nature of something being too much or too overwhelming for an individual to handle. In other words, the person experiencing the stress does not have the vitality to manage the problem, thus feeling crushed in the process.

If there is not enough energy or flow, there is often an undesired consequence. This is true at every level. Consider, for example, if a certain body part does not get enough oxygen or blood flow. That body part will become gangrenous, and if not removed, the disease will spread. Additionally, many accidents have been caused simply by exhaustion or sleep deprivation. If people do not rejuvenate sufficiently, they make mistakes or cannot respond appropriately to situations, thereby creating even worse problems.

On a more social level, if two people meet, and they are experiencing very different energy levels, it will be hard for them to endure one another's company. This is rather unfortunate as the two individuals may have much in common, but their varying energy levels provide them with no firm platform on which to begin the relationship.

You may doubt this to be the case. However, consider situations when you are very tired and very low on energy. If a colleague or acquaintance suddenly enters your space as bubbly and enthusiastic as a firecracker, you might tense up like a hedgehog; or your blood might begin to boil slightly, and you will think there is something wrong with you. You will have no idea whatsoever as to why you suddenly felt tense or irritated.

On the other hand, if you have very high energy levels and someone you know has very low levels (and might be feeding off yours), you might feel drained speaking to them. These people are colloquially referred to as "energy vampires" (DiGiulio, 2018). Even though you would like to be kind or empathetic to them, when talking to these individuals, you will realize that energy is a very precious resource.

This is the crux of it. Energy is a resource, and lacking this precious resource can result in very costly mistakes. With plenty of it, energy can be a catalyst for many successful ventures, beautiful friendships, and simply general well-being. With that said, humans have a complicated relationship with energy.

Think of physical activity. Many people exercise to increase their energy levels and promote healthier sleeping patterns. Since exercise requires a great deal of energy to perform in the first place, the immediate reaction is for people to feel very tired afterward. Yet, hours later, their energy levels remain consistent, and they are able to sleep far better.

According to Mathew Walker, sleep is a crucial ingredient in maintaining one's concentration and diligence. While sleeping, you also burn calories, creating potential energy. That is why sometimes when you wake up in the middle of the night, you'll notice that you've worked up a sweat. Ironically, at the same time, doing passive activities such as binge-watching Netflix may result in a decrease of energy. Even though watching TV is ultimately relaxing, you are not burning very many calories

(DiGiulio, 2018). Thus, potential energy is not being created.

It all comes down to energy. To say that there is an energy crisis in our modern world is an understatement, and calling it burnout or stress does not get to the root of the problem. However, naming it a disaster in energy gets to the bottom of the issue.

Unfortunately, one of the biggest issues getting in the way of solving this problem is living in a material world and having a material mindset. Though mentalities are changing with the expansion of psychology and psychotherapy, as well as the surge in popularity of mindfulness and mediation, many people believe that problems have a material nature. However, this is not often the case.

For example, while major financial difficulties cause people much pain and suffering, giving them an abundance of wealth will not end their problems. A clear example of this is the fact that 70% of lottery winners go bankrupt after a short length of time (Lottery Winners Who Blew the Lot, 2020). Getting rich overnight did not solve their problems, and actually, years later, they faced even worse circumstances; their financial prosperity caused rifts in their relationships with their loved ones.

Living in a material reality means we also concentrate on the visual aspects of the world and pay little attention to other senses, such as how a situation feels. We know how we feel when we are deprived of sleep, urgently seeking coffee for a boost. Later in the day, when we need a bit of a spike again, we might suddenly notice a bar of chocolate and gobble it up, waiting for the next boost. We see the chocolate and we see the coffee, but we do not try to feel what our body is telling us.

This is a huge issue with the material world. Coffee and chocolate, which come with a daily price tag, are very visually transfixing. Our body craves energy, but these two things are simply quick fixes. If we want to solve the crisis in energy, we need to take a step back and really get to the origin of the issue.

∾

MIND, BODY, AND SOUL

When initially dealing with an energy crisis, we have to consider the exact nature of energy. Where does it come from? Where do we feel energy?

On a purely physiological level, our bodies obtain energy from mitochondria in our cells. Mitochondria use calories, oxygen, and other nutrients to power cellular processes. In other words, the mitochondrion in each cell generates power for our whole body (Mitochondria, 2014).

However, we are hardly conscious of the millions of biochemical reactions happening in the millions of cells in our bodies. The experience of vitality occurs chiefly in a psychological manner. Thus, though we acquire energy from cellular processes, our psychological awareness is the only true way we have contact with our energy.

For instance, when you deal with stress and burnout, you are struggling with an obstacle to your mental vitality. In the case of stress or anxiety, often extremely paralyzing thoughts and worries tend to override your mind, making you feel unable to deal with a problem. The problem or problems (as stress and anxiety tend to occur when many issues are occurring simultaneously) seem overwhelming— much bigger and greater than you can handle. It goes without saying that psychologically, one feels hopeless and paralyzed not simply because of the existence of the problems, but because they do not believe they have enough strength to overcome the simultaneously occurring issues.

Lastly, as many of the world's societies have moved away from religious ideologies and adopted more secular visions, the concept of the existence of a soul or spirit has been overlooked. Admittedly, a trend is developing among New Age philosophers and thinkers such as Sam Harris to focus on spiritual aspects. In this way, a modern resurrection of spirituality is gaining ground. This revisiting of spirituality has been responsible for the discovery of new ideas and approaches to well-being such as the rise in the practices of meditation, mindfulness, and energy healing. As the trend shows, attaining happiness and healing from physical and psychological issues essentially has a spiritual tendency.

As we often overlook the importance of spirituality and its connection to energy, consider the word "inspiration" and the phrase "human spirit". Both contain the root "spirit". Sometimes, we tend to confuse the words "mind" or "psyche" with the word "spirit". However, the spirit needs to be distinguished from the notion of mind. Modern thinkers such as Robin Sharma have made this very distinction.

Sharma made this very profound statement: "The mind is a wonderful servant, but a terrible master". This indicates that people are not their minds. As opposed to the mind, the spirit can be characterized by its ability to overcome negative thoughts, destructive patterns and mindsets, and harmful biochemistry and perspectives. This is often why when people firmly decide to change the course of their lives, they are able to rid themselves of bad habits, harmful lifestyle choices, and self-destructive attitudes. Thus, having a healthy spirit is key in making necessary and also unprecedented changes to our lives. This importance should never be understated.

This is where Reiki comes in. Reiki focuses on energy healing in all three areas—our bodies, minds, and souls. One is not superior to any other; they are all integral to our vitality. Vivacity in one often entails strength in another. It is for this reason that any serious form of healing has to consider recovery for all three. Reiki is one of the few forms of therapy that does just this. This is why Reiki is not only holistic, but essential.

～

WHY REIKI?

Reiki may seem like a counterintuitive approach to dealing with physiological and psychological issues, but sometimes things appear counterintuitive because they are deeply intuitive; thus, we are no longer conscious of them.

For example, when you suddenly become very stressed, tense, or annoyed, one of your first reactions is to sigh deeply. Sighing is an involuntary reaction to negative feelings. It is also an indication that someone is experiencing stress, tension, or irritation. Unconsciously, what you are doing is trying to expel negative energy. Additionally, you are also trying to inhale fresh air to increase the flow of oxygen; and that new, fresh air makes you feel more invigorated.

This is what people are doing in a more extreme manner when they exercise. They are trying to optimize flow and reinvigorate themselves with more oxygen (and fresh air), creating better blood flow and increasing energy. Like reiki, exercise is also almost counterintuitive. Every day, people need to encourage and push themselves to exercise, but the goals remain the same: optimize flow and promote a surge in energy.

We looked at another example earlier. When you rest your face into your hands, you are instinctively searching for energy. As children, we may have gotten into the habit of doing this, but now we have become unaware of how this act automatically revives us.

In the modern world, we have grown out of touch with our intuition, so much so that intuitive practices seem absurd or ridiculous. Some of us do not even believe a soul exists, yet we are on a continuous search for inspiration and motivation. It is only now, when we are facing alarming rates of suicide (Suicide Statistics, 2020), depression, burnout, and stress (Elflein, 2016), that spiritual healing and the revitalization of energy do not appear all that ridiculous.

Reiki for Beginners is a guide to help you start your journey with the life-changing practice of Reiki. It intends to introduce you to the three levels of Reiki: Shoden, Okuden, and Shinpiden. While taking you through each of the levels, this guide aims to help you master energy healing using Reiki. Furthermore, it will help you understand the history and theoretical aspects of this practice while assisting you to master the various hand positions, Reiki levels, and meditation so that you can begin healing yourself.

Although this manual is not meant to be an exhaustive study on Reiki, it does intend to take you through the three levels to help you extend this therapy to your loved ones and others in your community. As there is an energy crisis in our modern dog-eat-dog world, enhancing one's energy can be likened to a spiritual wealth—one that is very much lacking but that is very much in demand.

CHAPTER 1

WHAT IS REIKI?

"Even though the body appears to be material, it is not. In the deeper reality, your body is a field of energy, transformation, and intelligence." –Deepak Chopra

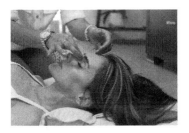

UNDERSTANDING REIKI

Essentially, Reiki is healing with energy. It is an alternative and holistic form of healing that relies on meditation, hand positions, and increasing one's flow and energy to soothe physical ailments, provide mental wellness, and increase spiritual vivacity.

To first understand Reiki, you can study its etymology. Reiki is a Japanese word. If you break it down into its two roots, you get *rei* and *ki*. *Rei* means "universal" while *ki* translates to "life energy" (Newman, 2017). Thus, Reiki is a practice that tries to provide healing through increasing the flow of energy to areas of the body or mind. Alex Bennet provides more insight into understanding the term ki.

The Japanese word *kti*, from which the word "Reiki" is formed, is the essential life force—the energy and warmth radiated by the living body, human or animal. Everything that is alive contains and radiates ki; when ki departs the living organism, life has departed (Newman, 2017).

As mentioned in the introduction, if the flow of blood or oxygen to a specific body part is disrupted, first this body part will not be able to function, then gradually it will die. This is not only true on a physical level, but in mental and spiritual dimensions as well. For example, when you are overwhelmed by angry and bitter thoughts, you do not stop being angry and bitter, but instead become even more so. It takes perspective and calming thoughts to dispel such negativity.

This echoes Martin Luther King's famous quote, "Darkness cannot drive out darkness; only light can do that. Hate cannot drive out hate; only love can do that" (King, 1963, p. 37). King's statement is not only virtuous but also logical. In a physical dimension, this also happens to be logical. If your foot is not receiving blood, what you do is increase the blood flow to it so it can heal; you do not continue to prevent blood flow.

Reiki incorporates this logic into its practice. If you are tired, weak, or suffering from physical pain, you need to optimize energy flow to a specific area. The same occurs with ki, or life energy. Bennet helps to elucidate this point: "Since ki nourishes the organs and cells of the body, supporting them in their vital functions, the disruption of ki brings about illness" (p. 2). Since humans are primarily composed of energy, Reiki can help not only physical impairments, but those of a metaphysical nature as well.

Having said this, mastering Reiki is simple, but it is not easy. It necessitates learning mediation, practicing various hand positions, and understanding the nature of energy. Currently, there are only about a thousand Reiki masters worldwide (Reiki, 2019). While the practice offers numerous physical and psychological benefits, it is technically a discipline. This guide aims to familiarize you with Reiki and help you begin your journey in learning this discipline.

∼

ORIGINS OF REIKI

When people first study Reiki, they come across the name Mikao Usui. Although Mikao Usui is formally responsible for founding this alternative form of therapy, Reiki takes its roots from much older philosophies and bodies of knowledge. In this sense, Mikao Usui's role can be described as formalizing Reiki into more cohesive and integrated healing methods based on ancient teachings. Therefore, anyone who wishes to begin a comprehensive and well-informed study of Reiki needs to begin with Buddhist Qigong.

Buddhist Qigong is a subdivision of Buddhism that developed four thousand years ago in China. As the spiritual philosophy is so ancient, it is arguably older than Buddhism, deriving from ancient Chinese philosophy, way of life, medicine, and tradition. Nevertheless, after Buddha's fame became recognized and spread throughout Asia, Buddhist Qigong rose as a subculture of Buddhism.

One of the hallmarks of Buddha's life that greatly influenced Buddhist Qigong, leading to its creation, was Buddha's talent for healing his followers and others who he encountered. In general, the Buddhist way of life concentrates on healing through various methods, namely meditation, improving one's karma and leading to exploration of the layers of the mind and of Reiki.

C. Pierce Salguero supports this point with the following comment:

Practical tools for mental and physical healing—

including but not limited to meditation—were adapted and elaborated across virtually all of Asia for most of Buddhism's history, and indeed have often played a major role in the popularization of the religion in its new host cultures (Paging Dr. Dharma, 2016).

As Buddhism became recognized for its ability to restore people's good health through its practices, many people across the continent of Asia were attracted to its success. In our modern world, it can be difficult to acknowledge what kind of impact Buddha's work would have had. In ancient times, medicine was largely primordial, and people back then suffered greatly from disease, lack of basic sanitation, and poverty. Consequently, the healing by Buddha's practices was a necessity many people could not do without.

Having said that, Qigong and subsequently Buddhist Qigong are derived from traditional Chinese medicine, which continues to be practiced in the contemporary world, as well as from other philosophies such as Confucianism and Daoism (Qigong, 2020).

When Buddha's influence became more prevalent in Asia, traditional Qigong and Buddhism developed a set of practices that would create the practice of Reiki. What distinguished Buddhist Qigong from other divisions of Qigong was its concentration on mind and spirit as the basis of healing (How to Tell, Buddhist or Taoist or Confucian Qigong, 2017).

Like with other forms of Buddhism such as Theravada, Mahāyāna, and Vajrayāna, during Buddha's lifetime and long after his death, Buddhist Qigong became widespread in influencing the way of life in Asia. It was in Japan where Mikao Usui formalized Reiki from the age-old customs of Qigong and established it as practice.

As stated earlier, while Mikao Usui is recognized as the founder of Reiki, this is rather misleading as it suggests that the technique of Reiki did not exist before him. Usui's own words imply something of a similar nature: "Reiki does not belong to one person or one community, but it is the spiritual heritage of all humanity (Who Is Mikao Usui And The 3 Things You Have To Know About Him, 2020).

What Mikao Usui can be credited with is mastering Reiki, refining it, formalizing it into a structured practice, and sharing this with the world.

Mikao Usui

Mikao Usui was born in 1865. When he was four years old, he began living in a monastery studying Tendai, a division of Mahayana Buddhism. During

Usui's time at the monastery, he became interested in world religions, psychology, and medicine (Who Is Mikao Usui And The 3 Things You Have To Know About Him, 2020, para 3). Naturally, it was his training in psychology and medicine that initiated Usui's path in energy healing.

The Richard Ellis School of Reiki offers insight into Usui's calling. It was during 1888 that he contracted cholera as an epidemic swept through Kyoto. He had a profound near-death experience during which he received visions of Mahavairocana Buddha and received direct instructions from him. This was a pivotal experience for Usui that caused him to make a major reassessment of his life. He developed a keen interest in the esoteric science of healing as taught by Buddha, and he developed the compassionate wish that he might learn these methods in order to benefit mankind (The History of Reiki 1865 - 1926, 2011, para 5).

Therefore, it was Usui's own close encounter with death that encouraged him to seek alternative healing techniques. The following few years, Usui devoted his time to pursue medical knowledge, causing him to diverge from Tendai. Usui soon became attracted to Shingon Buddhism, a division of the religion that solely concentrates on Tibetan Buddhism and the scriptures of Buddha himself (The History of Reiki 1865 - 1926, 2011). It was Usui's time in a Shingon monastery in Kyoto that facilitated his proficiency in energy healing and the establishment of energy healing as a practice.

The period between the late nineteenth and early twentieth century in Japan was a particularly catastrophic time. There were several epidemics that occurred, including another cholera outbreak, this time spanning twenty years. Also, in 1923, an earthquake took place causing a great deal of destruction to Japan and Yokohama (Who Is Mikao Usui And The 3 Things You Have To Know About Him, 2020, para 26).

Though these catastrophes severely impacted the Japanese people, Usui became dedicated to his people. He used Buddhist learning, his own experience overcoming cholera, meditation, healing through physical touch, and energy to help the Japanese nation. According to Reiki Scoop, Usui passed on Reiki teachings to roughly 2,000 people and assisted 13 individuals in becoming Reiki masters (Who Is Mikao Usui And The 3 Things You Have To Know About Him, 2020, para 32).

Hawayo Takata

Mikao Usui can be credited with creating a national awareness of Reiki, but it was Hawayo Takata who exported this practice to the world—first to the USA and later to the rest of the globe.

Takata's journey with Reiki began when she first received healing from Chujiro Hayashi's Reiki clinic. Chujiro Hayashi was a maritime officer who studied under Usui, eventually opening up his own clinic in Japan. At the time, Takata was suffering from a bladder disease from which she was told she would die. It was at Hayashi's clinic where Takata was able to fight her disease. Amazed by her own complete recovery, in 1936, Takata decided to learn the art of Reiki (Bennet, p. 4).

After training for two years, Takata journeyed back to her motherland of Hawaii and opened numerous of her own clinics, training others to be practitioners. From that point onward, Reiki became an international practice (Bennet, p. 4).

~

Reiki and Modern Popularity

It could be argued that the contemporary world is undergoing a kind of reformation or a revisit of ancient pools of wisdom. Eastern traditions, religions, and philosophies are growing in popularity all over the Western world. Suddenly, everyone seems to have an interest in yoga, mindfulness, and Vipassanā meditation (Kisner, 2020, para 2).

The core belief systems of Daoism and Buddhism have become very valuable exports to the West. They have also become digital. It is a unique meeting point for ancient customs and modern civilization. Reiki is one such practice that has surged in use.

Some reasons for the increase in Reiki's interest include contemporary issues such as burnout, stress, depression, and anxiety. Furthermore, as Reiki offers a holistic approach, many people are drawn to its ability to provide a remedy for physical ailments, but at the same time, aid people in finding mental endurance and energy. In a very secular world, we are discovering daily that many problems are not simply material but spiritual in nature. Thus, Reiki is a reasonable alternative as it concentrates on spiritual cleansing.

Jordan Kisner's article in *The Atlantic* gives more insight into the rising demand for Reiki:

Disillusionment with established medicine has been mounting for decades, fueled by the rising costs and more depersonalized care that have gone hand in hand with stunning technological advances and treatment breakthroughs. Eastern medicine and holistic healing models provided attractive alternatives to what critics in the late 1960s called the 'medical industrial complex', and by the new millennium extramedical "wellness" had become big business (Kisner, 2020, para 19).

Reiki has come a long way. While it may have begun a hundred years ago in a remote area in Japan, its export to Western countries has allowed numerous patients to receive the treatment while allowing scientists to study the results of the therapy. Scientific data has seen positive results on patients receiving Reiki treatment weekly (Reiki popularity growing, 2015). As there has been much success, many people are now turning to Reiki to help them manage everything from chronic pain to insomnia and fatigue. In recent years, the practice's surge in popularity has now been fueled by YouTube videos and blogs. Consequently, Reiki has been given a new life.

Every day, individuals in remote areas can learn this art without leaving their homes. As YouTube videos, blogs, and books are written about the practice, the more universal healing can be obtained. Not only do the prospects of Reiki look promising, but perhaps we can expect general wellness to spread and become a global phenomenon.

REIKI MEDITATION

Meditation constitutes one of the core components of Reiki healing. As Reiki is developed from Buddhist tradition, meditation is a significant feature of the practice. Meditation is an umbrella term for various kinds of mind training and spiritual cleaning. Reiki meditation is one variety. While every form of meditation has its own goals, the objective of Reiki revolves around energy. As the core of Reiki healing rests on the concepts of rei and ki, central to Reiki meditation is experiencing specifically the universe's energy.

This is not accomplished easily. Ramya Achanta provides more insight into the process of learning Reiki meditation when saying, "It involves symbols and mantras to facilitate your meditation experience" (Reiki Meditation – How To Do And What Are Its Benefits?, 2017, para 4). The symbols Achanta refers to are explained in the various levels of Reiki, while the mantras alluded to are the five Reiki principles. As we cover Level I, we will name these five principles as the next chapters are more concerned with the application of Reiki.

Reiki meditation also varies in structure compared to other meditation practices. For example, mindfulness meditation often entails the repetitive technique of clearing one's head of their thoughts. It can be described as a kind of tug-of-war between one's concentration and one's rebellious mind. On the other hand, Reiki meditation follows the process of cleansing, channeling energy to the chakras, healing through hand positions, and ending the session (Achanta, 2017).

In this sense, Reiki meditation differs from other kinds of meditation such as Zen and Vipassanā as it integrates the application of hand positions into the session. Thus, the practice is composed of two parts. In the next chapters, we will look at how to put this into practice.

Reiki meditation also varies from other kinds of meditation because it can be performed by an individual on themselves or by a person on another individual. Typically, meditation aims for individuals to have no contact of any kind—verbal or physical—with another person.

Yet, as the hands have so much healing power, this kind of contact is welcomed in Reiki, for it is through one's hands that one can transfer energy and open the chakras. Andrea Ferretti discusses in the article "A Beginner's Guide to the Chakras" how various yoga positions incorporate hand positions to open the chakras to help release tension and overcome physical pain.

～

SIGNS REIKI IS FOR YOU

Many people get involved in a kind of "pharmaceutical web". Adam Rostocki calls this the "pharmaceutical trap". First, it begins with something like insomnia. You treat your insomnia with zolpidem but are unaware of the side effects. Although you may read about the side effects in the pamphlet, you are still likely to continue medicating your insomnia with zolpidem. At the same time, your anxiety is likely to increase.

You become worried that you cannot sleep or are becoming dependent on a drug to induce sleep. As a result, you are now suffering from anxiety. If your anxiety becomes too unbearable, you may have to get treatment for it or seek professional therapy. Additionally, long-term use of any drug impacts your other organs, so while solving a problem now is necessary, other long-term ailments will surface.

Sadly, your insomnia goes untreated. You may have medicated your insomnia, but you have not actually solved the issue. Insomnia may sound harmless, yet current data shows there is a sleep crisis. The Good Body reports that "about 30% of American adults have symptoms of insomnia" (Insomnia Statistics, 2018, para 2).

While you may not be struggling with insomnia specifically, there could be other issues that may be preventing you from living a fuller life. These ailments can be physically or mentally related. However, often people do not receive Reiki treatment as they are not aware of the signs. Below are some issues that Reiki healing can help with.

- Fatigue: Reiki improves flow throughout the body, so if you are suffering from constant extreme exhaustion, this could be an issue with the flow of energy throughout your body. A certain chakra may be blocked or there might be tension preventing the stream of energy from reaching certain areas, thereby depriving you of energy (5 Signs That A Reiki Cleanse Would Benefit You, 2019, para 4).
- Stress: As mentioned in the introduction, stress is a feeling of not being able to handle certain pressure or a crisis. It is not solely the pressure or disaster that is the problem but rather that you do not have the strength to get through it. Once again, it may be due to an issue with energy circulation. To manage stress, Reiki can help you get the necessary strength which, in turn, balances your emotions (5 Signs That A Reiki Cleanse Would Benefit You, 2019, para 6).
- Inability to concentrate: While an inability to concentrate implies fatigue, it could also hint at an emotional imbalance. As with stress and fatigue, Reiki aims to discover the source of imbalance and redirect the flow of energy to that area. Since fatigue

can be likened to an absence of energy, the inability to concentrate can suggest an imbalance. Something you are not aware of is pulling your concentration all the time. Crystal Palace Osteopaths refers to these things as "emotional disturbance[s]" (5 Signs That A Reiki Cleanse Would Benefit You, 2019, para 7). With Reiki, you can discover the source of the emotional disturbance and what is usurping all your energy. Once you get to the bottom of it, you can redirect energy to other areas, such as your mental attunement, to assist with concentration.

- Depression: Depression bears some similarity to stress. While stress makes an individual feel overwhelmed and incapacitated so that they experience worry and anxiety, depression causes feelings of nihilism and submission. This is due to the individual's lack of physical strength and emotional resilience, all originating from insufficient energy. The key to healing a complex disorder such as depression is giving people resources— namely energy and confidence—to manage the crises and obstacles in their lives (5 Signs That A Reiki Cleanse Would Benefit You, 2019, para 8).
- Pain: Generally, pain is associated with tension. A specific body part might not be

getting enough energy supply, causing an energy blockage. In the case of pain, generally the blockage will have been occurring over a long duration. If a specific area is causing you discomfort, Reiki sessions will target that area, supplying energy once more to provide relief (5 Signs That A Reiki Cleanse Would Benefit You, 2019, para 5).

The above are a few examples of how Reiki aids people around the world. It is commonplace for people to suffer from these ailments or disorders globally; however, few people will ever realize that the source of their problem is insufficient energy flow. In fact, as scientists have discovered that humans and all life forms are composed of energy, it is no wonder that inadequate energy supply can have devastating impacts on our spirit, mental alertness, and physical forms.

CHAPTER 2

SHODEN: USUI REIKI LEVEL I

"Reiki gently brings our spiritual journey into focus and increases the natural flow of events and patterns of manifestation in our lives." –Linda A. Rethwisch

SHODEN: USUI REIKI LEVEL I

Reiki is a three-tier practice. When starting your Reiki journey, you begin with Shoden, which is Japanese for "first teachings". There are three sections of Shoden, and in each segment you cover a unique Reiju. In Usui Reiki Level I, trainees and patients are introduced to the chakras and the concepts of Shizen Joka Ryoku, the body's natural cleansing system, and Byosen.

Reiju

A Reiju is a ritual or spiritual blessing usually received in one session. This "spiritual blessing" entails the Reiki practitioner creating a safe area around the patient, thereby allowing the patient's ki to flow. Though Reiju is a ritual, no physical performance occurs. Frans Stiene of The International House of Reiki gives more information on the nature of Reiju:

Mikao Usui was 'just sitting' as the Great Bright Light, encompassing the entire cosmos and being that space of open possibility. In that space, Usui could offer the Reiju as a healing, a blessing, an initiation, or all at the same time. In that space, the student could receive whatever he or she needed, at that moment in time. There was no need for ritual; only the ability of the person 'giving' the Reiju to be the Great Bright Light (Stiene, 2012, para 3).

During a Reiki session, a Reiju can be performed by the Reiki master to begin the process of healing. The Reiju primarily involves sitting in the presence of the master to experience the universe's energy. During this ritual, it is crucial for the patient to feel this universal energy as it allows their ki to flow (Reiju and Attunements, para 3).

However, if an individual is in a Reiki training session to be a Reiki practitioner, they would need to obtain a minimum number of Reiju. As there are three sections of Reiki Level I, the trainee would need to acquire three of the different spiritual offerings from the master. Furthermore, the trainee would have to keep learning to recognize and observe the universe's energy.

In your training to be a Reiki healer, it is essential

to meditate on universal energy and life force. While meditating, try to experience how energy flows through your body when in a sitting position. Meditation is one of the key practices you can use to feel this life force. Therefore, it is essential to be in a completely silent environment which also has little activity. If there is too much movement in the area, you will be distracted from sensing your own innate energy flow.

Chakras

The notions of chakras and auras hardly need an introduction as these entities are well understood internationally. That said, no guide to Reiki would be complete without discussing the chakras and aura. When receiving a Reiki treatment, the master will concentrate on the chakras as these are the main energy openings. There are seven chakras that are aligned starting from the individual's crown down to the end of their spinal column.

In the list below, the seven chakras will be named, and a brief explanation will be given of each of their functions:

- Sahasrāra chakra: the crown chakra
- The Sahasrāra chakra is considered the "source of light" as it enhances your spiritual connection with a "higher being" (Sahasrāra Chakra, 2019, p. para 1). As this chakra links with our higher selves, in Buddhist and Hindu philosophies, it is the most important of all the chakras.
- Ajna chakra: the third eye chakra
- The Ajna chakra relates to rational or clear thinking, reflection on the internal and external world, and contemplation on one's self (Third Eye Chakra - Ajna).
- Vishuddha chakra: the throat chakra
- The Vishuddha chakra is associated with speech and communication. When unblocking this chakra, it enhances a person's ability to communicate honestly and openly with themselves and others. Transparent conversation with oneself is considered just as important as an honest conversation with the external world (Vishuddha Chakra: The Throat Center, 2020).
- Anahata chakra: the heart chakra
- The Anahata chakra is the heart chakra. It is associated with love, connection, warmth, and empathy. While this chakra is our core to extending kindness and compassion to others, if we are hurt by others in romantic relationships or carry

the pain from negative social interactions, our heart chakra can become blocked. Thus, unblocking the Anahata chakra is key to not only releasing such pain, but to helping us to build solid relationships again.

- Manipura chakra: the navel/solar plexus chakra
- The Manipura chakra is situated by the navel and solar plexus. On a physical level, it relates to digestion and metabolism, while metaphysically it is associated with our ambitions or intentions (Snyder, 2017).
- Svadhishthana chakra: the sacral chakra
- The Svadhisthana chakra is located by the lower pelvis. As it is close to the groin area, there is a distinct connection between the Svadhishthana chakra and intimacy. It is necessary to transfer energy to this chakra to assist with emotional balance in deep relationships and to provide healing to reproductive functions (Synder, 2017).
- Muladhara chakra: the primary/root chakra
- The Muladhara chakra is positioned by our perineum, the edge of our spines, after our coccyx. It is our primary chakra and associated with foundation and stability. For example, if you damage your coccyx, you will not be able to walk. Therefore, unblocking the Muladhara

chakra is essential for performing all
tasks.

If you intend to become a Reiki practitioner, it is
crucial to always concentrate on clearing or opening
the chakras. Many of the hand positions, which we
will discuss in Chapter 5, provide healing to the
patient, with each one focusing on a different area.
An obvious example is one of a Buddhist monk
sitting in the lotus position with his or her hands
pressed together in front of their heart. The hands in
this area allow the universal energy, ki, to be directed
specifically to the Anahata chakra.

As a prospective healer, it is necessary to take
time and give special care to each hand position for
every one of these chakras as they are the founda-
tions of an energy healer.

Shizen Joka Ryoku and Byosen

Shizen Joka Ryoku is the intrinsic function every
body has to heal itself. This is not limited to animals
only, like dogs or cats who lick their wounds to clean
them; the human body also has this capability.

A clear illustration of this is when our white
blood cells attack foreign and harmful pathogens that
enter our systems. Unconsciously, our systems are
alerted, and the white blood cells come to our
defense. Another example is if something damaging
goes straight into your eye; your eyeball immediately

begins to water to flush out the foreign invader. While we all know such things thanks to biology lessons at school or university, we tend to forget about the body's innate healing system.

However, it is arguable that we do *not* forget. When many of us get sick, we do not seek a medical consultation with a doctor immediately since we know that if it is nothing too serious, our bodies will be able to overcome the ailment. Besides, since most issues are primarily blockages of energy, if we can direct our internal energy to our chakras or areas that are suffering from tension, even healing chronic illnesses is possible. We are simply relying on the body's natural healing function.

Another principle to Reiki Level I is Byosen Reikan Ho, the removal of toxins from the body. When preparing for their first attunement, Reiki masters ask patients to avoid consuming alcohol, caffeine, sugar or nicotine prior to the session. In order to completely cleanse oneself, it is essential that there are no harmful chemicals in the body as it will impair the healing (Reiki Attunement - The Process and Purpose). Additionally, the patient is encouraged to let go of negative thoughts such as resentment and bitterness as this too will negatively impact the attunement process (Reiki Attunement - The Process and Purpose).

While Reiki concentrates on opening the chakras and evenly distributing one's life force, Byosen Reikan Ho is concerned with removing negative energy and toxins. In Reiki Level I, trainees learn about Byosen Reikan Ho, but in Reiki Level II, prospective Reiki practitioners need to apply this knowledge of the first level. Thus, only a simple introduction of Byosen Reikan Ho is necessary. In the next chapter, we will look at the practical components of Byosen Reikan Ho.

SHODEN: PRINCIPLES

When a student begins their journey with Reiki, they are taught five mantras, or philosophies. These are referred to as the Reiki principles and students are expected to apply them to their lives every day. The five Reiki principles are as follows:

- Just for today, I will be grateful.
- Just for today, I will not anger.
- Just for today, I will not worry.
- Just for today, I will do my work honestly.
- Just for today, I will respect all life (Who Is Mikao Usui And The 3 Things You Have To Know About Him, 2020, para 33).

One should not simply repeat these principles but try to meditate on and embrace them throughout the day. By integrating these mottos, Reiki becomes similar to a way of life. Meditating on the five principles helps one to build a connection to their meaning and the gravity of each mantra.

As with mantras in general, there is power behind the words. For example, if you berate yourself, you are likely to use words such as "fool" or idiot" or call yourself stupid. When you say these words, they have an innate power or vibration. Unfortunately, the power in these words is likely to impact you negatively, making you feel weaker.

On the other hand, consider words such as "calm" and "transcend". They are powerful for different reasons. They too have intrinsic energy to them, and when you repeat them to yourself, you feel better and channel more positive vibrations.

The Reiki mantras above relate to the core purpose of the practice—they intend to restore one's energy and give one the strength to cope with trauma or catastrophes. If you analyze the first mantra "Just for today, I will be grateful", concentrating on the word "today" minimizes one anxiety and helps a person to condense their energy to what they can handle. On a separate note, much of Buddhism centers around being present for this helps the individual to focus on what is tangible and, consequently, in their power to really control.

When performing a Reiki healing session, the patient is asked to repeat the mantras. Try wording them so that you can feel the calming energy each one inspires. Furthermore, when saying them to yourself, note how you reserve your strength for today and relinquish control over tomorrow. In other words, you direct your energy to the day.

MODERN ADAPTION AND POPULARITY

As mentioned in the introduction, Reiki has become digitized. While it is possible to receive Reiki healing through a video or podcast—and many teachers have provided this service online—it is recommended during your first Reiki attunement sessions to opt for a physical session. However, as there are always limitations with distance and time, it is possible to go online for this service.

The same is true if you intend to become a Reiki healer. It is advisable to learn the practice through its physical application. In the presence of a Reiki practitioner, you can see all the various steps taken during a session. Similar to a healing session, there is Reiki Level I content uploaded by institutions such as the International School of Reiki. If you do feel face-to-face classes will be more useful, there are many schools offering the same service. Usually, these organizations offer training in Reiki I, II, and III, so they can be worthwhile.

SHODEN: LEVEL I AND ATTUNEMENT

As Shoden is the first level of Reiki, much of the training is devoted to learning about the origins of energy healing and understanding how Reiki works. Much of it is theoretical, and we covered this in the introduction. Furthermore, in Reiki Level I workshops, you also learn about chakras, the five Reiki principles, Shizen Joka Ryoku, and Byosen.

Once you are finished learning the theoretical background, you can have your first attunement. You will need to receive your attunement personally from a Reiki master. The Reiki master can begin the session with a Reiju to open the patient to the universal energy (What Is A Reiki Attunement And Why Is It Necessary To Get One, 2020, para 4). The master will sit in a deep meditative state, concentrating on getting the patient to experience the universal energy.

Stillness and silence are imperatives throughout the session. Next, the Reiki master may introduce the student to the five Reiki principles or the Reiki I symbols. The patient needs to focus on the power of these words when repeating them as they are not simply words, but carry innate vibrations helping to draw negative energy out.

Next, the healer will search the body for any points of tension or blocked chakras where the flow of energy has been stalled. Such areas might be physical, like a knot in the back where tension has been building up. There could also be a similar problem with the heart chakra, where energy is not flowing too well. The problems may be physical or emotional. Heart pain is associated with emotional suffering and physical ailments such as Mitral Valve Prolapse (MVP).

The Reiki healer will press their hands onto the areas showing tension or build-up, or just below or above the injured areas (What Is A Reiki Attunement And Why Is It Necessary To Get One, 2020, para 38). This is done to open the channel for energy to the area. Sometimes, the practitioner will also press down on the tense area. Remember, to prepare for your first attunement, you need to rid your body of all toxins, including caffeine, alcohol, negative emotions, bad habits like watching negative TV programs, and self-destructive thoughts (Reiki Attunement - The Process and Purpose). Throughout this part of the session, the patient will keep their eyes closed.

As Reiki masters have varying methods of performing a Reiki attunement, they differ in length. One session could be five to fifteen minutes in length. Some masters include a prayer and meditation as part of the session, so it might take longer (What Is A Reiki Attunement And Why Is It Necessary To Get One, 2020, para 40). It should be noted that before one can be a healer, they need to receive a Reiki attunement. This is to ensure that the universal energy can be transmitted from the practitioner to the patient.

After Attunement

After their first Reiki attunement, many people experience different reactions. Penny Quest describes some reactions patients have felt after this attunement:

After an attunement is over, students often describe the beautiful spiritual or mystical experiences they have received, such as "seeing" wonderful colors, visions, or past life experiences. Others report receiving personal messages or profound healing, sensing the presence of guides or angelic beings, or simply having a feeling of complete peace. Some people go through a real shift in their awareness immediately afterward, describing the sensation as almost like being reborn, so that they experience everything around them more intensely—colors are brighter, their sense of smell is enhanced, and sounds are sharper (Quest, 2003, para 1).

Thus, responses include heightened sensitivity, healing of pain and tension, increased tranquility, relief from stress, and spiritual visions. On the other hand, there can be adverse effects post-attunement. You may experience symptoms of physical cleansing and detoxification such as a runny nose, headaches, or diarrhea. The more toxic you are, the more symptoms you may notice. There is no need to be alarmed, though; the body is simply flushing out the toxins (What to Expect During and After a Reiki Attunement, 2020, para 2).

Furthermore, sensitivity is also increased. However, it should be noted that this is sensitivity to both positive and negative feelings and sensations. Thus, while you may laugh intensely and experience deep love for everything, you will also become more affected by light, colors, and touch. These are common after-effects. As some people have more toxins in their bodies, they will feel much more sensitive post-attunement.

21-DAY PURIFICATION

Generally, patients are required to go on a 21-day detox after an attunement process. There are several steps one needs to follow during the 21-day detox:

- Perform a self-cleansing on oneself for five minutes every day

(In Chapter 5, hand positions will be discussed, and you need to perform a self-healing on yourself selecting the most appropriate one).

- Regularly drink water, keeping yourself hydrated.
- Eat plenty of fruits and vegetables, and avoid processed foods.
- Try to meditate, or do yoga or movement meditation.
- Sleep about eight to nine hours every night.

The purpose of the 21-day purification is to continue the spiritual and physical cleansing of the body. It complements the attunement session with the master. As mentioned above, cleansing of any form does often involve adverse effects. Thus, if you do experience extreme sensitivity or headaches, it simply indicates your cleansing is effective.

REIKI LEVEL I

Reiki Level I is composed of learning the background of Reiki, learning what Reiki is, and understanding Byosen, Shizen Joka Ryoku, the five Reiki principles, and the chakras. If you are interested in becoming a Reiki healer, you will also be introduced to some hand positions that are used for energy healing. To move on to Reiki Level II, you will need to understand very well what Reiki is and how it works. Furthermore, the various theoretical concepts mentioned above such as Byosen and the chakras are covered in more detail in Reiki Level II, but theoretical comprehension of these notions is essential in Reiki Level I.

You will also need to have an attunement session with a Reiki master. Though only one attunement session is required, it is advisable to have additional ones to deepen your spiritual cleansing and promote the flow of your ki (Learning Reiki).

For patients, attunements offer deep cleansing. However, prospective practitioners require familiarity with the universal energy and need their own ki to flourish in their bodies before they can provide spiritual cleansing to another. The 21-day detox is equally important. During this period, it is essential to perform a self-healing treatment once a day. This is for both patients and future healers.

This chapter sought to introduce Reiki Level I to readers. It covered the basics common in this level. However, different institutions vary in their approaches. Some introduce Reiki symbols during Reiki Level I, while others do not. To complement your application of Reiki Level I, you will need to use the hand positions provided in Chapter 5.

Lastly, while Reiki Level II concentrates on more self-healing and healing others, if you would like to use this guide to simply heal yourself and not advance to Level II or III, that is perfectly acceptable. In this case, it is recommended that you go over hand positions next.

CHAPTER 3

OKUDEN: USUI REIKI LEVEL II

"All healing is first a healing of the heart." –Carl Townsend

OKUDEN: USUI REIKI LEVEL II

The second tier of Reiki is Okuden. In Japanese, Okuden means "inner teachings". While Shoden Level I focuses on theoretical backgrounds, Okuden explores some other concepts but also initiates the prospective healer with the practical process of healing. Similar to Shoden, there are also spiritual blessings (Reiju) and attunement sessions which are separate from your classes should you wish to become a Reiki practitioner. In Usui Reiki Level II, the training covers the drawing of Shirushi (the Reiki symbols), Seiheki Chiryo Ho, the development of intuition, the application of Byosen, and Jumon and mantras.

. . .

Reiju

Some training courses offer two spiritual blessings, but there are others that provide three. Once
again, every Reiki center is different; some are more
intensive and in-depth. In recent times, Reiki training
for one level can be conducted over a day, so
throughout that day, the Reiki teacher will transfer
these Reiju to the students. For example, courses
offered from Alternatively Better and Epona Equine
Reiki Centre take place over a day.

In Shoden, the Reiju the Reiki healer transfers to
the patient or student aims to introduce the
universe's energy to the receiver. As passing the
Reiki Level II grants the Reiki practitioner the ability
to perform Reiki healings on others (Classes), the
prospective healer needs to become deeply familiar
with sensing the universe's energy.

Right now, It may seem daunting as a potential
healer to read this, but it is recommended to have
one's first Reiju and attunement in person with a
Reiki master. As this is a spiritual sensation that
occurs, there are no exact theoretical indicators.
Having said that, since energy is being transferred to
you, one of the indicators is a sense of revival or reju-
venation. This can occur in a spiritual, creative, physical, or even emotional form.

Nevertheless, it is difficult to explain to a person
what happens after they receive Reiju. It should also
be noted that after this spiritual blessing is given to
you from the Reiki master, you have received it. The
connection with the universe's energy is now within

you, and you can transmit it to a loved one or patient.

∼

SHIRUSHI: REIKI SYMBOLS

One of the aspects which embodies Reiki is an emphasis on visualizing and then drawing specific symbols. As mentioned earlier, Okuden means "inner teachings" in Japanese. What makes these teachings "inner" is that they are hidden (Reiki Level 2 | OKUDEN – What To Expect From It And Its Symbols, 2020, p. para 1). In other words, the notions of Reiki concentrate on entities that are characteristically internal. They are so internal, in fact, that they remain "hidden".

There are three to five core Shirushi. Some schools teach all five, while others focus on only three. James Deacon explains that it is possible that the Mikao Usui only used two symbols in the original Reiki training (More Concerning Reiju, 2005, p. para 2). It was probably when Hawayo Takata exported Reiki to the west that more symbols were incorporated. While there are varying numbers of symbols, it is specific to the institution. One possible explanation for this is that some courses span one day, two days, or six months. Thus, there is more time to learn about each symbol and practice visualizing and drawing it.

. . .

The Power of Symbols

Symbols are sources of power. While they are basic pictures (like hieroglyphics), each image is charged with not only meaning but energy. This might sound odd to you, but throughout the world, certain symbols have the power to create strong emotional reactions or oblige you to do something.

Symbols have meaning. Meaning is a part of their nature. Road signs are symbols with simple meanings. Some symbols have a deeper meaning. They are a powerful gate to the deeper and less conscious levels of human experience. Symbols evoke profound emotions and memories—at a very primal level of our being—often without our making rational or conscious connections. They fuel our imagination. They enable us to access aspects of our existence that cannot be gotten to in any other way (The Power of Symbols, 2017, para 5).

Consider pictograms of a water drop or the Christian cross. The water drop does not only represent water, but a source of life, a drinking hole, vitality, nature, and now, that your device is waterproof. Concerning the Christian cross, it takes influence from the Egyptian Ankh, and thus, has survived close to eight thousand years. The Christian cross has intrinsic meanings like the "key of life" (Ankh - Egyptian Symbol of Life, 2015), faith, managing the burden of life (the crucifixion), or believing in Christian values (Cross, 2020). The connotation is so entrenched with the pictogram that it is hard to remove the meaning from the symbol.

If someone from Italy wore a Christian cross, even those from distant lands such as China or Japan would be able to associate the meaning of the cross with Christian values. It is the same as a water drop. If you showed someone a picture of a drop of water in various countries around the world, people would be able to make similar inferences as to its meaning, such as the source of life, vitality, and nature.

Moreover, symbols are logos, too, or rather, there is no real difference between a logo and a symbol. Usually, logos are associated with brands, but the intention behind them and symbols remain the same —they represent a specific association as well as its products, services, and values.

Symbols are not simply pictures; they fuel our society. Traffic signs manage the coming and going of vehicles while pictograms of a basic design of three stairs indicate a fire escape and where to go in an emergency. Furthermore, symbols transcend time. Their power does not always end with the death of a civilization, as is the case with the Egyptian symbol of the ankh, which has survived the ancient Egyptian kingdom, continuing through Christianity 8,000 years later.

The Power of Reiki Symbols

Reiki Symbols

Cho Ku Rei

Sei He Ki

Hon Sho Zo Sho Nen

Dai Ko Myo

Da Koo Mo

Raku

Though the pictograms of Cho Ku Rei and Da Koo Mo are associated with Reiki, they derive from ancient traditions. In Reiki, Shirushi are considered sacred as they connect you with a hidden energy, only released on contemplation, visualization, and reproduction of the symbol. Reiki Scoop provides more insight into the nature of symbols: "Each of these symbols acts like a key that unlocks "hidden" energy. This is just a comparison, of course, but the idea stands. They connect to a certain energy, vibration, and manifestations of the universal life force" (Reiki Level 2 | OKUDEN – What To Expect From It And Its Symbols, 2020, p. para 45).

In Takata's Reiki teachings, the internal power within each Reiki symbol was explained. Each one holds a unique power concentrating on a specific source of energy. However, in general, each symbol revealed Reiki philosophy.

The Five Level II Shirushi

- Cho Ku Rei: the power symbol
- As it represents "universal energy", Cho Ku Rei is considered the primary symbol of Reiki. The "coil" in the symbol is seen to be the universal meditator (Price). Its intersection depicts the channel or path to that universal energy. Like with Reiju and the basic concepts of Reiki, channeling the universal energy is said to bring healing and cleansing (Reiki Level 2 | OKUDEN – What To Expect From It And Its Symbols, 2020). Thus, when visualized and drawn, the power symbol helps a person to make a connection with this universal energy, bringing about their healing and cleansing.
- Sei He Ki: the calming symbol
- According to Natasha Price, "Sei He Ki has been interpreted as meaning 'God and man become one' or alternatively 'the earth and sky meet', both referencing the connection between two elements, the conscious or mental body, and the subconscious or emotional body" (Price, Universal Symbols: The Calming Sei Hei Ki, 2019). In the

pictogram itself, an interplay between two figures can be seen. While there is a split between the two, it should also be noted that they complement and run parallel to one another. These two figures represent "man" and "divinity" or "body" and "spirit". In this sense, these two entities are in constant interaction with one another, but they also complement each other. In other words, they are dependent on one another. Reflection on Sei He Ki can help an individual first ponder on the necessity of balancing their emotions and mind, spirit, and body; however, it can also help the individual to attain this balance. Continuous meditation on this symbol assists a person in feeling tranquility with all the various aspects of their being aligned and stable.

- Hon Sha Ze Sho Nen: the distance symbol
- In Japanese, Hon Sha Ze Sho Nen means "no past, no present, no future" (Price, Universal Symbols: The Distant Healing Hon Sha Ze Sho Nen, 2019, p. para 1). Deep contemplation of this symbol allows an individual to transfer healing beyond time. In this sense, Reiki allows healing and cleansing to transcend time. Price provides more information on this process: "By using the Hon Sha Ze Sho Nen symbol, we become one with the energy which flows through us and across all time

and space" (Price, Universal Symbols: The Distant Healing Hon Sha Ze Sho Nen, 2019).

- Shika Sei Ki: the heart-healing symbol
- In the previous chapter, we analyzed how if your heart chakra is blocked, you can experience numerous issues. This can include emotional problems such as loneliness, heartache, and reluctance to love, or they can be physical in nature, such as heart or chest pain. To complement opening the heart chakra, you can meditate on, visualize, and try to reproduce Shika Sei ki. Pinky Punjabi wrote the following on healing through this symbol: "This symbol is best used for heart-related diseases or also for people undergoing emotional stress in life. [It is] one of the most amazing symbols for anger-related issues. This symbol eliminates negative energies from the heart, giving way to unconditional love" (Punjabi, 2015).
- Shika So: the throat chakra symbol
- Shika So and Shika Sei Ki are usually learned in tandem as they both focus on deep emotional cleaning and healing. Reflection on Shika So relates specifically to difficulties in expression, throat pain, and thyroid issues. Unblocking the throat chakra can reduce tension in this area and

aid with giving the individual relief from the above problems (Punjabi, 2015).

When you are first introduced to the Reiki symbols, you will learn what they are, how they function, and why it is essential to reproduce them, either through visualization or reproduction.

Visualizing

Visualization of the five Reiki symbols requires a lot of mental exertion. Though it can be exhausting to create an exact replica of an unfamiliar symbol, this process is key in uncovering the hidden power of the five Reiki symbols. Cho Ku Rei is an easy one to begin with.

First, imagine an infinite spiral that is intersected by an upside-down L. By reproducing this pictogram in your mind, you are creating a conscious association with the universal energy. Furthermore, when visualizing the spiral, concentrate on its infinite nature, and thus, its abundance. When you think of the upside-down L, recall how this is the universal energy's channel within you. It intersects at Sahasrara, your crown chakra, and continues down this path, traveling to every chakra.

During meditation or your 21-day cleansing, try to concentrate on picturing the five Reiki symbols. If you can only manage to focus on two or three, that is fine too. Remember that for many Reiki training programs, you are only required to learn three Reiki symbols.

As with Cho Ku Rei, while imagining a spiral and upside-down L, try to create associations with other images so that you can accurately envision the symbol. When you do manage to form a precise reproduction, visualize it for a couple of minutes so that you build a stronger link to it.

Drawing

In Usui Reiki Level II sessions, time is allowed for students to draw these symbols. Websites such as Reiki Scoop teach their followers techniques for how to draw them accurately. If you think of the sacred symbols as a series of lines and circles, it can simplify the process of drawing them.

While drawing recreates tangible images, the physical process of reproducing these pictograms helps to cement them in your mind. It also allows the power of the Reiki symbols to enter a physical realm. You realize they are not only for mental well-being, but for physical relief as well.

Sei He Ki manages the complementary relationship of physical and emotional well-being. It is no simple feat to accomplish a balance between these two. Yet creating a tangible representation of Sei He Ki allows you to actively remember that this balance is a necessity.

The main objective of drawing Reiki symbols is to integrate them into the healing process itself. When you begin to use Reiki remedies to restore energy, drawing the symbols on areas inflicted with tension provides relief to these regions. For example, if you are struggling with loneliness, reproduce the image of Shika Sei Ki over your heart chakra to open it to the energy of the universe.

Not only is there the power of physical touch that provides healing to this area—perhaps your emotional dis-ease is also creating tension in the region of the heart chakra—it also reminds you of the love your highest being unconditionally bestows upon you and the abundance of love across the world.

While drawing this symbol on your heart chakra, remember the nature of love. There is no one person, nation, or society that has a monopoly over love. Love is universal. Like with this example of drawing Shika Sei Ki over the heart chakra, try to do the same with the other chakras.

You may not be suffering from feelings of loneliness or isolation, but perhaps you want to acquire the ability of free communication and meaningful expression. In this case, you can practice drawing Shika So over the throat.

～

SEIHEKI CHIRYO HO

Seiheki Chiryo Ho takes the initial spiritual cleansing received in Reiki Level I further. As with the spiritual detox in preparation of the attunement and for the 21 days after this healing, this concept tries to cement good habits and establish attainable goals for a person (Seiheki Chiryo Ho, 2006).

While Reiki primarily concentrates on healing through universal energy, it also endorses maintaining one's physical health. Reiki, in fact, seeks to balance emotional wellness and mental vitality with physical well-being. In other words, spiritual growth is not superior to physical vigor but rather equal to it. With this in mind, Reiki intends to improve the individual's well-being by encouraging good habits and establishing goals for its patients to obtain. For instance, many patients attend Reiki sessions to help them quit smoking (How Meditation and Reiki can help you stop smoking, 2020) or to assist them in finding direction in life (Fleming, 2018).

In the section on hand positions, we will look at the practice of implementing Seiheki Chiryo Ho so that you can begin to lead a life of good habits and clear direction.

DEVELOPMENT OF INTUITION

There are two misconceptions that should be clarified before discussing Reiki and its objective of developing an individual's intuition. First, many people believe that intuition informs them of when they are doing something wrong or protects them from something that will harm them. This is true, but intuition also tells us when something is right for us or will benefit us. The problem with this is that we think of the "gut instinct" as helping us to avoid adversity and negativity, as opposed to leading us to experiences of positivity. We do not typically believe it can direct us to opportunities or relationships.

Oftentimes, we pay attention to what our intuition says about people who have wrong intentions for us. Though we may not act on it, we still listen to what our instinct is saying to us. On the other hand, when we feel a very strong connection to someone, in order to save face, we might not encourage the relationship or shy away from establishing a further connection.

The second misconception about intuition is that it is unreasonable or illogical. When we discuss the various kinds of knowledge, we believe there are analytical and intuitive types. By saying that intuition is not logical implies that it is unreasonable or even wrong. In the introduction, we spoke about many processes that are so deeply ingrained in our habits and customs that we do not even recognize that they exist. For example, to feel a child's forehead is a form of being able to tell if they suffer from illness (Bennet).

If your mother or grandmother felt your forehead after you said you were feeling feverish, you would not think it nonsensical. It has been a reliable method of figuring out if a person has a fever since before we developed thermometers. Intuition is a reliance on ancient habits that have become instincts through centuries of practice. These instincts or this kind of knowledge is so ingrained that we need not reprocess it on every occasion.

In Reiki Level II, you reflect on the significance of sharpening your intuition as well as how to apply this intuition when becoming a practitioner. As with a fever, you use your hand to tell if someone is sick or not. While heat may be an indicator of infection or inflammation, if an area is also too cold, it is not receiving enough energy or blood flow. These are some of the signs you look out for as a Reiki healer.

It is also important to note that not all your instincts will be logical or reasonable. You may not have consciously figured the logic out. Therefore, developing your intuition remains a significant feature to improve if you want to be a Reiki healer.

APPLICATION OF BYOSEN

The instincts addressed in the previous section are relevant to applying Byosen. For Shoden, you study the notion of Byosen, and for Okuden, you learn how to practice it.

Toxins are harmful to our bodies. They cause a variety of health issues. A build-up of tar from smoking can prevent easy breathing and affect oxygen supply. Fat droplets in your blood cells can result in blood supply being lost to that area, which ultimately is responsible for heart attacks and gangrene.

When practicing Byosen, search the patient's body for any of these signs showing there may be a build-up of toxins, which include the following:

-The area is cold: This may indicate that there is not an even supply to the region.

-Lack of pulse: Once more, this implies a lack of an even supply.

-Heat: The area is above the general temperature of the body.

-Pain: If the healer touches the area, there is some sensitivity.

-Tingling: If the patient feels a pins-and-needles sensation, it may indicate toxins in the area (Petter, p. para 2).

The more serious the affliction, the more time is needed with the injured area. For example, if two or more of the above symptoms appear in that region, the higher the number of toxins. Or if one symptom is very advanced (e.g., if the temperature is dramatically higher than the rest of the body), then once again, you will want to spend more time healing that region (Petter).

When beginning the Byosen treatment, Petter describes the process: You place your hands on that area and feel the Byosen. If you feel a strong Byosen, such as level four or five, you know that something serious is happening there that needs possibly time-consuming attention. As you hold your hands on this area, you should pay attention to the peaks and valleys of the Byosen. It comes and goes in waves (Petter).

It should be noted that when practicing Byosen on someone, if the symptoms appear very advanced, it is strongly advised to seek assistance from a medical professional or Reiki master. As you are still in training and gaining experience in this form of healing, it is better to do this in more serious cases.

JUMON

In Usui Reiki Level I, the Reiki student was introduced to the five Reiki principles. There are some training programs which teach these principles, mantras, and Jumon at the same time. We will not go through the five Reiki principles again, but we will look at Jumon and mantras as well.

Mantras and Jumon are quite similar. James Deacon explains that mantras can be single words or phrases with an intelligible meaning. In other words, mantras are repeated words or phrases with a meaning understandable to the speaker. Jumon are also words or phrases, but they serve more as chants or incantations that focus much more on the sound and, as a result, the vibration of those sounds. Deacon explains that Jumon is "a mystic, spiritual or magical incantation—a 'spell'—a sacred phrase or invocation".

The Jumon used in Reiki have mixed origins. Some originate from Buddhism and Taoism, while others are from Shintoism. Over the years, their pronunciation has changed slightly.

Jumon for Usui Reiki Level II:

- *a ba ra ha kya*
- *watari no fune*
- *qu xie fu mei*

Similar to mantras, when saying these words, try to concentrate on the sound that is created by each syllable. The art is in repetition. First, pay attention to trying to reproduce each syllable. When you have mastered the individual sounds, then try to repeat the phrase several times, listening carefully to the sound of the sequence and the vibration it produces in your mouth, as well as after it leaves your mouth.

As opposed to mantras, where the power is derived from the language and meaning of the words or phrases, Jumon creates power from the sound and vibration produced by the word. Jumon is part of Usui Reiki Level II as it composes one of the "hidden", or "inner", teachings.

~

OKUDEN: ATTUNEMENT AND 21-DAY PURIFICATION

Once you have finished learning about Shirushi, Seiheki Chiryo Ho, intuition, Byosen, and Jumon, you will be ready for your next attunement. As with your first attunement for Shoden, you will need to prepare for this process with a detox. You should abstain from harmful chemicals such as nicotine, alcohol, caffeine, and sugar. If possible, try to avoid eating red meat and incorporate as much fresh fruit and vegetables into your diet as you can.

Once again, you will also need to detox spiritually, letting go of harmful thoughts and negative emotions. As with the Shoden attunement, you will also need to visit a Reiki master to receive the Reiju and attunement for Okuden.

During the attunement session, the Reiki master will concentrate on helping your body circulate the universal energy by unblocking the chakras and removing toxins and pathogens. Every attunement session brings about different responses, so you may feel highly sensitive, much lighter, or far more energized. Reactions are both positive and negative— negative because you have begun the process of removing toxins and pathogens. After the attunement session, you will begin the 21-day purification process.

21-Day Purification

Generally, patients are required to go on a 21-day detox after an attunement process. Take a look below at the steps one needs to follow during their detox.

- Perform a self-cleansing on oneself for ten to fifteen minutes every day.
- Keep yourself hydrated by drinking lots of liquids.
- Maintain a diet eating chiefly fresh fruits and vegetables.
- Meditate, practice yoga, or do movement meditation.
- Get enough sleep (about eight to nine hours each day).
- Practice drawing the symbols.
- Repeat the Jumon incantations.
- Practice healing others by using Byosen, drawing the symbols on injured or afflicted areas, and helping others build good habits with Seiheki Chiryo Ho.

MOVING ON TO REIKI LEVEL III

As mentioned already, training courses from different Reiki centers follow unique structures, so you may attend a Reiki institute that covers the symbols in Level I while only going through the five Reiki principles in Level II.

Before you move on to Shinpiden, you will need to study the various sections discussed in this chapter, and you will also need to receive two or three

Reiju and at least one attunement—although it is possible to do more than one. There must be a period of 21 days spent on the purification process to prepare you for Shinpiden.

Okuden focuses on "hidden", or "inner", teachings. The art of Byosen, the meditative reflections on Shirushi, and the development of one's intuition all concentrate on hidden or internal knowledge. In this sense, Okuden is essentially intuitive. It forces students to pay attention to sound, vibration, and the signs of toxic manifestations in the body. Once you complete Reiki Level II, you are ready to heal those around you and move on to Usui Reiki Level III.

CHAPTER 4
SHINPIDEN: USUI REIKI LEVEL III

"Energy and persistence conquer all things." – Benjamin Franklin

SHINPIDEN: USUI REIKI LEVEL III

Shinpiden is the final phase of Reiki training, and upon completion, you will become recognized as a Reiki master. *Shinpiden* is Japanese for "mystery teachings". In Usui Reiki Level III, the "mystery teachings" assist the prospective Reiki master in attaining enlightenment or discovering their true self (Exploring Mikao Usui's Teachings, 2014).

During this training, you will learn the necessary master healing techniques and will be given the resources to follow the path as a master. Techniques that you learn include Holy Fire or placement attunement, Healing Fire ignition, and master ignition, as well as how to conduct an attunement on yourself and others. Resources also include the Holy Fire symbols necessary to be a Reiki master. At the end of the training, you will look at ethical codes of conduct and practices for a Reiki master.

One thing should be noted before continuing with Shinpiden; while anyone can participate in Shoden, Usui Reiki Level III is reserved for astute students and healers. While this may seem slightly demotivating, you need not feel discouraged. Past Reiki masters include Buddha and Jesus (Bennet). Jesus was famous for his ability to heal. Considering his accomplishment of raising Lazarus from the dead, Jesus was a very skilled Reiki healer.

Thus, with regular practice, meditation, and visualization exercises, you can learn to become adept at Reiki and continue with Shinpiden training.

SHINPIDEN: HOLY FIRE OR PLACEMENT ATTUNEMENT

In Usui Reiki I, you received your first Reiju and experienced your first attunement session with a Reiki master. The moment the Reiki master transferred the Reiju and universe's energy to you, you gained these gifts. You spent Reiki II learning about various techniques to equip you as a Reiki healer, and now you need to integrate what you learned and harness the gifts of Reiju and spiritual cleansing so that you can begin to heal and teach others.

Before offering attunement sessions to others, you need to practice attunement with yourself and setting up the right conditions so you can experience universal energy. Reiki centers such as Balance on Buffalo recommend practicing for about a year before you begin with others (Reiki Master Attunement, para 1).

Setting up an Attunement Session

To set up an attunement session, you need to find a quiet and calm environment (Reiki Master Attunement). If there is too much activity, it will lessen your ability to feel the universe's energy. Try to avoid any movement, music, or conversation being in the room. It is true that conversation and movement all are created from the universe's energy, but what you need is a direct channel with the universe.

- Place a candle in the room, and invite energy into the space with the three steps.
- Attitude of gratitude: "I thank Reiki, all the masters, and myself.
- Use your fingers to draw the Reiki II symbols.
- Invite Reiki into the room: "Reiki, you are

kindly invited into the room to do the
attunement process for (patient's name).

- Bow to the patient (if you are the patient, bow to yourself so you can channel the universal energy to yourself).
- Take a deep breath.
- Ask the patient to take a deep breath and relax.
- Say thanks to the universe (Reiki 1 Attunement Process, 2020).

Meditation can be an easy way to center yourself and align yourself with the universe's energy. In the beginning, when practicing on yourself or on loved ones, you can meditate for five or ten minutes before the session. On another note, there may be bird or traffic sounds around you. Remember that this is also activity derived from universal energy. If you concentrate on these sounds and this motion while meditating, it allows you to recognize how you are one part of this great whole.

Try to practice attunements on yourself. When you are comfortable, you can offer this healing to your family and loved ones. Furthermore, having more attunement sessions with a Reiki master can aid you in attuning your senses to your ki. If you are interested in becoming a Reiki healer, then familiarizing yourself with the attunement process is vital. With that said, you could also practice this in your own time. Just remember to set up your attunement environment before each session.

HOLY FIRE/MASTER IGNITION

Holy Fire is a type of healing Reiki masters can perform on one's spirit. While the topic of spirit has become controversial, which is discussed more extensively in the introduction, Holy Fire ignition is not affiliated with a religion. However, this healing does concentrate on providing cleansing for spiritual ailments, namely when trying to free the patient of their ego. Reiki Maya explains how a Holy Fire healing is different from attunements.

The Reiki master only has to call upon Holy Fire Reiki, and the energy will come and work with every student, attuning them to Reiki. This is without the need of performing the physical attunement. This process is named "ignition". It is at the forefront of how Reiki is evolving, becoming an "ego-free" process (What is Holy Fire Reiki?, 2019, para 2).

While an attunement tries to connect an individual with the universal energy so that they can be revived from its force, Holy Fire ignition aims to restore a sense of humility in this individual. This is counterintuitive to the overall message media and marketing gives us, yet freedom from the ego and a sense of humility can be not only liberating, but rejuvenating.

The Ego

Many popular contemporary writers and thinkers such as Ryan Holiday, Tom Bilyeu, and Alain de

Botton are realizing the benefits of creating a distance from the ego. An interview with de Botton describes this process: "It's about a surrender of the ego—a putting aside of one's own needs and assumptions—for the sake of close, attentive listening to another, whose mystery one respects, along with a commitment not to get offended—not to retaliate—when something 'bad' emerges, as it often does when one is close to someone, child or adult" (The School of Life: An Interview With Alain de Botton, 2019, para 17).

Besides these obvious benefits, liberating ourselves from our egos is also crucial in bettering our relationships with ourselves. For example, when you are going through a good phase in your life, you experience a form of hubris, which is the arrogance of all arrogances (Hubris, 2020). You have an elevated level of pride and flatter yourself continuously.

However, at the same time, an internal voice—perhaps, the voice of your "true self"—warns you that things can change very suddenly and advises you against being overly confident. Later, when things do eventually go wrong, you berate yourself, pull your self-esteem to pieces, and say very unkind words to yourself.

In both situations, it is the ego that is in control. First, the ego seduces you with imagined self-importance, then it pulls you to pieces using the most destructive vocabulary imaginable. What is most important is that your ego stands in the way of you discovering your true self.

Mikao Usui realized how the ego was an obstacle in finding one's true self. In this sense, the Holy Fire ignition is centered around eliminating the ego's hold over the individual. By using the universe's energy, the hold of the ego is diminished, the spirit cleansed of its hubris and destructive nature, and a path to realizing one's true self is illuminated.

A Holy Fire ignition, also known as an "igniting the fire" ceremony, can only be performed by a master. It is fundamental as a Reiki master to first attend a Holy Fire ignition and then perform their own.

SHINPIDEN: ATTUNEMENT

There are two attunements reserved for Level I. The first is the last of your attunements for Reiki training; this is a continuation of your attunements and purification processes of Level I and Level II. The second attunement is an induction into the attunement process, what techniques you need to incorporate, and how to conduct an attunement session to bring healing to others (Dai Ko Myo Reiki Master Symbol And Reiki Level 3 Shinpiden, 2020).

Once you have received your final attunement, next you need to concentrate on how to give attunement to others. Much time is dedicated to practicing attunement with others. You can only pass Reiki Level III if you have mastered this art.

Tips for Mastering Attunement:

- Self-exploration
- Shinpiden focuses on "mystery teachings". While we may believe we know ourselves deeply, we often question our motivations for things we have done in the past. Sometimes, we do not interrogate ourselves enough; we do not ask ourselves why we have certain prejudices, preconceptions, habits, or dislikes. "In the 'true sense', a Reiki master should be a mentor, professor, or trainer—an entity that

offers knowledge and wisdom and always seeks the path to enlightenment. You should always seek to work and improve yourself" (*Dai Ko Myo* Reiki Master Symbol And Reiki Level 3 Shinpiden, 2020). To be able to give someone else the energy of the universe, you need to have a deep connection with this energy. Being your authentic self is essential in acquiring this deep connection.

- Meditation
- The popularity of meditation should not be understated. It is one of the few times when a person is really alone with themselves. During meditation, a person has to confront what their mind is and how it works. While the practice may bring the worst parts of your mind to the surface, it also allows people to see the best of themselves, recognizing their higher beings. Furthermore, being in a still and silent environment helps you in witnessing and experiencing the energy of the universe.

You may be distracted by bird sounds, a hungry mosquito, or traffic sounds. Yet, if you can gently carry your mind back to your breath, you can realize your strength over your mind and thus, your ego. You will also acknowledge how the universe's energy is abundant. It is in everything—the birds, the hungry mosquito, and all the agitated drivers stuck in traffic.

Naval Ravikant sums up the necessity of meditation: "Meditation is intermittent fasting for the mind. Too much sugar leads to a heavy body, and too many distractions lead to a heavy mind. Time spent undistracted and alone, in self-examination, journaling, meditati[ng], resolves the unresolved and takes us from mentally fat to fit" (420 Naval Ravikant Quotes to Make You Happy [and Wealthy]).

- Practice
- This point has already been discussed at the beginning of this section. It needs to be reiterated that practice is essential in acquiring Reiki mastery. Nothing that comes easy is worth it. To become a Reiki master takes a lot of time, work, and determination.
- Review Reiki I and II materials
- The materials provided in Chapters 2 and 3 are the basis of Reiki. Many courses require you to pass tests and write papers to ascend to the next level. For an attunement, you will need to have a good grasp on the locations of the chakras and their functions. Take time to review Shoden and Okuden notes so that you are prepared for conducting a Reiki attunement.

～

SHIRUSHI: MASTER SYMBOLS

There are two symbols introduced in Usui Reiki Level III. While one institute may present trainees with both in the program, others may choose to only share the master symbol with those practitioners who become Reiki masters. During Shinpiden, there is more emphasis on becoming aligned with the energy and vibration generated from each symbol.

- Holy Fire symbol
- The Holy Fire symbol represents the concept of the Holy Fire discussed at the onset of this chapter. It is the surrender of the ego to the quest for enlightenment. When visualizing this symbol, the patient diminishes the ego's grasp over them. The pictogram of the Holy Fire symbol is a burning flame. Reflecting on this process helps to rid the patient's spiritual being of the negativity and toxicity produced by the ego.

- Dai Ko Myo: master symbol
- Dai Ko Myo is the gift of purest light or energy. When you are handed it, a direct channel with the purest energy is being created. The first pictogram depicts a kind of star with a vertical line being formed at a convergence. The vertical line reveals the channel that is being formed with the purest light. It is then distributed throughout your entire being through Sahasrara, the crown chakra. Thus, when trying to obtain this purest light, you will need to draw this master symbol on your crown chakra. As we mentioned in the previous chapter, visualization and drawing can help you perfect this skill. When you are not using an attunement practice or providing healing to yourself, meditating and reflecting on this symbol is not only beneficial, but necessary as a

master. Visualizing and meditating on it reminds you of the purest energy. It brings its power to consciousness.

RESPONSIBILITIES AND ETHICAL CODES OF A REIKI MASTER

Responsibilities

Being a Reiki master brings with it a lot of responsibility. Not only does it require daily practice, regular self-attunement, and leading a spiritually clean life, but you are also responsible for the physical and psychological welfare of others. However, to be a Reiki master, you need to learn many soft skills related to caring for others. The list below includes some of these aptitudes a master must acquire.

- The pursuit of knowledge must be your goal.
- Be kind and compassionate to all sentient beings.
- Be proficient in Reiki skills and obtain a great deal of Reiki knowledge.
- Feed humankind's spiritual hunger.
- Encourage love where it is possible.
- Be a bringer of light.
- Do not lie and motivate others to not lie.
- Heal people honestly and deeply.
- Guide others to live a life of sober habits.
- Always seek self-improvement (Dai Ko

Myo Reiki Master Symbol And Reiki Level 3 Shinpiden, 2020, para 7).

Ethical Codes

Like all medical professions such as dentists, doctors, and physiotherapists, you have an ethical code of conduct. These medical professions are in contact with people's bodies, and thus are working with individuals on an intimate level. It is of the utmost importance that you treat all people's bodies with respect.

The following are a list of codes that a Reiki master and healer should follow:

- Do not endorse any form of discrimination, and heal without prejudice.
- Always inform your customer or patient of the details of a healing session so they understand what to expect and make an appropriate decision.
- Maintain professional integrity.
- Do not disclose clients' private information unless asked by the law to do otherwise.
- Respect patients' bodies, and only perform energy healing through touch on areas that the patient consents to.
- Acknowledge all Reiki practitioners and support them as much as possible with

their training, but also treat them with dignity.

- Continuously update yourself on new Reiki regulations, and comply with all Reiki ethical codes.
- Strive to build a relationship of trust with all patients.
- Only provide treatment that has been certified by Reiki programs and courses which are offered by centers affiliated with the Reiki Association.
- If you receive criticism or a complaint, reply as soon as possible, and respond in an appropriate and constructive manner
- Recognize the importance of your position and responsibility as a Reiki instructor (Code of Ethics of the Reiki Association, 2020).

Lastly, there are some guidelines provided by the Reiki Association that can encourage transparency and professionalism:

- Display your Reiki certificates and qualifications.
- Offer patients thorough knowledge of their physical and psychological health.
- Try to avoid postponing or canceling appointments.
- Be considerate to all patients and colleagues.

REIKI LEVEL III

As the world of Reiki has become digitized, many organizations promise almost overnight ascension to master level. Unfortunately, this is too optimistic. Genuine graduation to the master level takes about a year after Okuden. Once completing Okuden, usually a student must spend another year or two practicing Reiki healing and reviewing its theory. Not only do you need throughout knowledge of Shoden and Okuden, but you require proficient capability in performing hand positions to master the Reiki techniques to provide healing to yourself and others.

Mastering Reiki is no walk in the park. It takes a lot of mental and physical exertion. Daily practice and meditation are necessary, as well as being an astute example of spiritual cleanliness. This entails maintaining a lifestyle where you avoid harmful chemicals and relinquish the hold negative emotions have over you. Furthermore, it involves a commitment to overcoming one's ego and being a keen-minded student who is always in favor of self-development and gaining new knowledge. These commitments remain constant even after one becomes a qualified Reiki master.

CHAPTER 5

HAND POSITIONS

"Our sorrows and wounds are healed only when we touch them with compassion." –Buddha

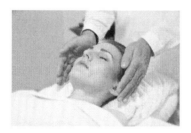

INTRODUCTION

The essence of Reiki is physical touch. The hands are channels through which energy is transferred to unblock tension or to restore one's innate ki. There are many other therapies that use physical touch through the hands to provide healing, such as massages, physiotherapy, and chiropractic work. While it is debatable, Reiki is the only practice that applies this form of healing to assist with psychological and emotional issues. However, if visiting a physiotherapist entails ending chronic pain and, as a result, restoring one's vitality, then one would suffer emotionally as well.

Furthermore, physical touch is not only used by medical professionals, but it is integrated into all cultures. Alex Bennet reveals this innate proclivity for physical touch:

Touching to comfort and relieve pain, or the laying on of hands, is as old as instinct. When humans are hurt, they immediately put their hands on the spot. A mother's touch or kiss provides soothing aid for a child's hurts. A mother's natural instinct with a sick child is to use her hand to feel for a fever. Animals immediately lick injuries and touch and lick their young as they learn. These simple acts form the basis for healing techniques through touch (Bennet).

Hands are the main tools for providing energy healing. They are one of our most valuable assets as humans. The number of functions they provide is limitless. For instance, hands clap to make sound, they wave to greet, the fingers on the hands can point, hands can massage to remove tension, they can balance us to stop us from falling or catch our falls, hands pray, and they are instruments of violence.

Hands are our sources of life and they can be instigators of death; and hands heal. They are some of the most powerful instruments we have. Their energy is immense. Think about how many other functions they perform. We cannot deny the intrinsic aptitude stored in our hands.

More than a hundred years ago, Mikao Usui must have recognized the sheer magnitude of their capabilities; he must have acknowledged the instinct of the hands to heal. Perhaps he noticed that when we suffer from stomachaches, the hands rub the belly to soothe the pain. Or maybe he saw that when people are worried about something, they often use their hands to cup their face. He most likely noticed that hand healing is instinctual and unconscious.

It is now time to revisit hand healing and to bring it into consciousness. In this chapter, we will look at the main and secondary Reiki hand positions to reassert the power of hand healing.

THE MAIN REIKI HAND POSITIONS

Below are the main Reiki hand positions. These are the main positions since energy healing is transferred to vital organs such as the stomach and kidneys, as well as the seven chakras. These hand positions can be utilized in both self-healing and healing to others.

- First position: the crown of the head

Putting both your hands on your crown draws energy to your crown chakra. As the crown chakra relates to your higher being and spiritual connection with the universe, this position optimizes flow to your higher self (What Are The Reiki Hand Positions And How To Use Them, 2020, para 3).

- Second position: the third eye and back of head

Put one hand on the forehand and one directly

behind it for this position. As this works with Ajna, it helps to clear the mind, sharpen mental acuity and memory, diminish stress, and revitalize mental endurance (What Are The Reiki Hand Positions And How To Use Them, 2020, para 3).

- Third position: hand over eyes

Allowing your hands to gently cover your eyes helps to give your eyes a visual time-out and returns mental vitality. When you are exhausted or visually overwhelmed, this position can help to reduce the strain on your eyes and face (What Are The Reiki Hand Positions And How To Use Them, 2020, para 3).

- Fourth position: hand over ears

This particular position helps to prevent mental exhaustion by limiting information overload and by cleansing both brain hemispheres of excess information. Think about people who protect themselves from a loud noise; in a similar sense, we protect ourselves from receiving too much information (What Are The Reiki Hand Positions And How To Use Them, 2020, para 3).

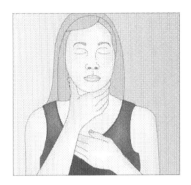

- Fifth position: the neck position

The neck is a very vulnerable area. Like our wrists and ankles, it receives a lot of contact, but is not always sufficiently supported. Furthermore, we tend to overstrain it nowadays with desk jobs. Place your hands around your neck to relieve the pressure. By easing the tension, you are also opening your throat chakra, or Vishuddha, to help you communicate effectively and express yourself more clearly (What Are The Reiki Hand Positions And How To Use Them, 2020, para 3). Wrap both hands around your neck, making sure that every finger has contact with the neck area.

- Sixth position: The center of the chest

This sixth position soothes Anahata, the heart chakra. This is a main Reiki hand position because it provides healing to a much-needed area. Daily inter-actions with people, both big and small, may cause a build-up of pain and resentment, ultimately creating a reluctance to socialize and love. Moreover, a healthy heart often entails a healthy body, so keeping the heart chakra relaxed and its energy restored results in long-term vitality. The chest area is not limited to the heart; it also supplies light and energy to the curve of our backs and our lungs. Two minutes of healing to this area every day promotes positive social interactions and healthy heart and lungs in the long run.

- Seventh position: the solar plexus position

There are many vital organs in this area that use a lot of the body's energy. (What Are The Reiki Hand Positions And How To Use Them, 2020, para 3). According to Reiki Scoop, these organs provide us with protection and essential life force. Spending two minutes doing this hand position can ensure you do not neglect those organs, though on a day-to-day basis, it is easy to forget they are there.

- Eighth position: the navel position

As this hand position works in the region of Svad-hishthana, or the sacral chakra, it deals with intimate, sensual, and intense relationships. Using the energy and light from your hands to heal this area aids the patient in having more meaningful relationships. It also can boost creativity. (What Are The Reiki Hand Positions And How To Use Them, 2020, para 3).

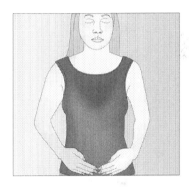

- Ninth position: the kidneys

Most people forget about their kidneys (unless you have kidney stones). On a daily basis, the kidneys work hard to remove toxins from and balance the chemicals in our bodies. They are the undervalued soldiers of our bodies. The eighth main reiki position ensures we spend a bit of time bringing relief to these organs. Reiki Scoop provides more insight into the eighth position: "Not only will healing here enhance the navel area energy center, but it will help you regain your daily energy and vitality as well as sustain and help the organs" (What Are The Reiki Hand Positions And How To Use Them, 2020, para 3).

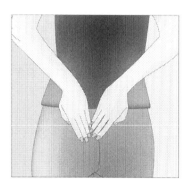

- Tenth position: the sacral area

In Chapter 2, we looked at the functions of Muladhara, the primary chakra. As this is our root, or primary, chakra, we need to ensure it is well-balanced and well-supplied with light and energy. The Muladhara provides us with stability and a firm platform on which to navigate and experiment with life. While other chakras, such as Sahasrāra and Ajna, seek to advance and discover, this is only possible if the individual is well-grounded and humble. Therefore, it is vital that constant attention is given to the sacral area to provide the individual with stability and a firm platform from which to grow (What Are The Reiki Hand Positions And How To Use Them, 2020, para 3).

THE SECONDARY REIKI HAND POSITIONS

The next positions are referred to as secondary hand positions. This is because they do not deal with major organs, but mainly limbs and appendages. Despite being secondary, many people struggle with pain in these areas. Though they are not the main positions, including them in a self-treatment or therapy session can help end discomfort.

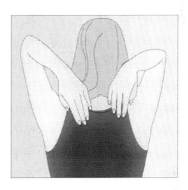

- Shoulders

As many of us have desk jobs or spend much time hunched over a desk, the shoulders tend to tense up, and consequently, light and energy cannot freely travel to them. After a week of tension or this block-age, the shoulders begin to suffer from a lot of discomfort and stiffness, and a person may need to go to a masseuse for assistance at that point. Additionally, Reiki Scoop explains that "when we carry a lot of emotional baggage, these two places tend to be tense and stiff" (What Are The Reiki Hand Positions And How To Use Them, 2020, para 4). Thus, providing daily relief can prevent long-term pain and prevent you from seeking aid from a masseuse, physiotherapist, and chiropractor.

- Hips

Our hips are deeply connected to our sacral chakra. Sexual, intimate, and intense emotional desires are stored here, often unexpressed (What Are The Reiki Hand Positions And How To Use Them, 2020, para 4). If there is too much build-up in this area, long-term issues could include a lack of enthusiasm for sexual intercourse and intimacy. Moreover, since the hips are some of the strongest bones in the human body and responsible for much of our movement and stability, soothing them daily or as often as possible can help promote more flexibility. This can, in turn, initiate more inspiration for intimacy.

- Knees

When you run, the shock of the impact as your foot connects to the ground is absorbed by the knees. This is not only true for running but for walking and movement in general. Many people endure injuries early on because of bad support and a lack of knee protection (Healthwise Staff, 2019). Cleansing and restoring energy to the knees ensures support for the rest of the body as we run, walk, and move.

- Feet and soles

Like our hands, our feet are involved in many activities that are fundamental for movement. This dependence on our feet means that if we experience discomfort in this region, it can incapacitate us. Going for a walk on grass can soothe this area, and so can this hand position. Not only does providing a remedy to this area help us to support our daily movements, but releasing stored up tension can get rid of stress and maintain better emotional balance (Burgess, 2018, para 3).

NOTES FOR HEALING OURSELVES

After Usui Reiki Level I, you are introduced to the main and secondary Reiki hand positions. Shoden training necessitates that you practice on yourself to learn these positions by heart (Reiki Hand Positions, 2014, para 1). This will also form part of your 21-day purification.

Try to set up a daily routine to perform a self-healing session. When starting out, try to spend time learning each of the positions. Also keep in mind that you know your body, so you know where there is tension and discomfort. When you move onto

Okuden, you will need to increase the time of your self-healing session so that you can perfect this process.

It should be noted that since your body informs you of where there is pain or a blockage, you should try to search your body for signs of toxins by applying the practice of Byosen. One more thing to remember is this: though your body tells you where there is discomfort, try not to neglect specific hand positions as you will need to be familiar with them during Okuden and when healing others.

NOTES FOR HEALING OTHERS

The Reiki Association has strict codes instructing how to provide healing for others. While during Shoden and Okuden training it is useful to practice on others, the Reiki ethical codes and values should be strictly adhered to. Always give your patient—even if it is a loved one—full knowledge of what the hand positions involve. It could be useful here to show them pictures of the positions so they know what to expect. Although you are now healing another body, you will apply the same hand positions to that person.

For example, the following are examples of hand positions for fifth and sixth positions being performed on others.

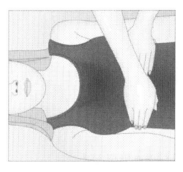

The hand positions are very similar but can be adapted for the patient. The patient will also be lying down to receive the treatment. When providing the treatment, be respectful of the patient's body, and always indicate before the treatment where the various hand positions are located so they know what to expect, once again, even if it is a friend or loved one. If a patient is uncomfortable during the process, energy will not be able to circulate freely, and it will disrupt the abilities of the energy and light to heal.

Lastly, ask the individual receiving the treatment

which areas are causing them pain (Code of Ethics of The Reiki Association, 2020, para 1). While it is necessary to rely on intuition and Byosen to know which areas to heal, patients also have a good idea of where they are experiencing tension or discomfort.

CONCLUSION

Our hands are wonderful instruments. Unconsciously, we are aware of their multifaceted nature, but we often forget that one of their intrinsic functions is to heal. On a primordial level, we use them to provide emotional comfort and support and to rub stomachaches or massage our temples. Many therapies rely on physical touch to promote healing, and Reiki is one such therapy.

If you put your hands to your face right now, you will feel their warmth and the energy vibrating through them. They are not simply energy, but light as well. Healing through the hands depends on using the internal energy and light in them to provide healing for a range of issues. Spending some time each day to learn the Reiki hand positions can be useful in providing long-term relief to discomfort, pain, tension, heartache, and loneliness.

This chapter served to discuss the biology of the hands and why they are so crucial to Reiki. The next chapter will briefly explain the main and secondary Reiki hand positions so that you can begin learning them by heart. Finally, it will list important reminders to make a note of before starting self-healing or healing others. Before you begin with self-healing and healing others, you must first master the Reiki techniques.

CHAPTER 6

MASTERING REIKI TECHNIQUES

"Energy is the essence of life. Every day you decide how you're going to use it by knowing what you want and what it takes to reach that goal, and by maintaining focus." –Oprah Winfrey

INTRODUCTION

Truthfully, this book has not followed a structured format. First, it has explained the theoretical under-pinnings of various Reiki practices. In most programs, at the end of each day, you will spend time covering the theory of a practice, then time will be dedicated to its application. For example, in Reiki Level I, you are usually introduced to some hand positions, and later, you will practice them in the training center and when you go home.

For the sake of compartmentalization, this book has taken a nontraditional approach, discussing each concept of Reiki in detail, then later teaching you how to apply Reiki methods. Having said that, in previous chapters, techniques were named for the visualization and drawing of Shirushi, and for preparing for attunements. However, these are primary techniques supporting much more advanced Reiki techniques. For instance, the ability to draw a symbol can be used to initiate a healing practice.

While meditating and visualizing Shirushi is an effective method on its own, it often complements other rituals in Reiki, such as meditation and healing through physical touch. This chapter will not cover those approaches for attunements and the visualizing and drawing of Shirushi; however, they will be referred to for the supplementary functions.

In this chapter, we will cover mastering essential Reiki techniques, namely Reiki meditation, mastering hand positions and Byosen, and Seiheki Chiryo Ho.

REIKI MEDITATION

The goal of Reiki meditation is to connect you with your divine element, to help you discover your true self, and to attune you to the universe's energy.

- Find a peaceful place in which to meditate. Similar to attunements, the external world needs to be as calm as possible so that you can be more sensitive to your internal life force and to the vibrations of the universe.
- Sit or lie down in a relaxed position.
- Take a deep breath, inhaling through your nose and exhaling through your nose.
- For the first two to three minutes, you can concentrate on your breath.
- Pay attention to it entering through your nostrils, sinking down into your lungs, and exiting through your chest.
- Deepen your inhalations so that you enter more deeply into relaxation.
- Try to get your breath to reach the pit of your stomach. (Note: it may be a bit forced now, but breathing into the diaphragm helps to increase the amount of breath you receive.)
- Once you feel relaxed, draw your attention to your mind.
- Send thoughts of loving-kindness and compassion to yourself. You can choose your own words or you can recite the following:

>I would like the very best for myself.

>I would like to make myself proud.

>I send myself love, kindness, strength, and compassion.

>The energy of the universe is in me.

You can also repeat the five Reiki principles during this meditation if you know them by heart.

When you are finished with the thoughts of loving-kindness, dispel any negative thoughts. During the last ten minutes, your mind most likely wandered once or twice to some knee-jerk bitter or angry thoughts; send them out into the universe. Perhaps, you may not have had any negative emotions but brought your mind to other distractions. You could have thought of the chores you needed to do or bills you had to pay. These thoughts can distract us during the mediation and cause anxiety and stress. Send them out into the universe as well.

- Next, place a hand on your seven chakras. Put your palm first on your crown, then your third eye, throat, heart, solar plexus, navel, groin area, and perineum.
  Remember, all the chakras are aligned, so

you need to move the palm vertically down the chakra path.

- Try to spend about 30 seconds to 1 minute on each area. (Note: if a specific area requires more attention, then you can spend longer channeling energy to it.)
- During the meditation, if you experience any discomfort, tingling, or pain, use the appropriate hand position to provide healing to that area.
- Continue to inhale through the nose and exhale through the mouth.
- Count to ten, and every time you count, inhale through the nose and exhale through the mouth.
- When you are ready, open your eyes (Achanta, 2017, para 3).

~

HAND POSITION STEPS AND TECHNIQUES

Steps

Whether providing healing through the hand positions to yourself or to others, it is vital to follow the steps provided below. You should follow these steps before, during, and after the healing ritual.

Before:

- Wash your hands first to remove all impurities and toxins.
- Declare to the universe's energy your wish to use light and energy to heal the patient's body (What Are The Reiki Hand Positions And How To Use Them, 2020, para 2).
- Rub your hands to channel light and energy to these regions, or you can use one of the Reiki symbols to open the hands to grant healing (What Are The Reiki Hand Positions And How To Use Them, 2020, para 2).

During:

- If you aim to perform a full cleanse, you can spend two to three minutes on each area. However, if you wish to target some specific areas that require attention, then you can ask the patient which body part is in great discomfort. In this case, you can spend five to ten minutes sending light and energy to the region.

- Place your hand on the area. When the area begins to relax, you can remove your hand. (Note: it is essential to develop one's intuition and knowledge of the chakras and to practice Byosen to fully know when to move on to the next area.)

After:

- Say thanks to the universe's energy.
- Inform Reiki, the universe's energy, that the session will end.

Techniques

There are different approaches to offer healing with the hand positions. They are beaming, cleaning, scanning, tapping, and swiping, which we go over below.

Scanning (Byosen):

We have extensively discussed Byosen in Chapters 1 and 2, so we will not explore scanning in great detail. The process of scanning the body for toxins and negative emotions is the first ritual performed during a Reiki treatment.

Scan the body for signs of toxins:

- Heat
- Extreme heat
- Lack of pulse
- Sweat
- Tingling
- Cold

Alternatively, you can ask the patient if there are pins and needles, sensitivity, or numbness in any area (Petter).

As you conduct your scan, your hands will locate a body part that has an excess of toxins. You can place your hands on the area or just below it. Sometimes, not placing a palm directly on the afflicted area restores its energy. If you do place a hand directly over the injured body part, you have a risk of suffocating the area or obstructing the flow of light or energy.

Beaming:

Rae Jae Reiki explains how beaming works:

A powerful method of channeling Reiki energy is called beaming. It can dramatically increase the amount of Reiki flowing through the practitioner to the client. Beaming also creates a unique healing process of treating the whole aura at once. After treating the aura, the Reiki energy will enter the physical body and treat areas that need it. It is also possible to beam Reiki directly to a specific area (Beaming, 2018, para 1).

Here is the process:

- The patient lies or sits down.
- The Reiki healer channels the universe's energy with sincere intention.
- They stand with their hands raised a couple of meters from the patient, then direct the universe's energy to the individual.
- It is sent to the patient's aura, entering at the crown, then distributed throughout the person.
- The healer needs complete concentration on the patient's healing (Giaser, 2020).

Cleaning:

Cleaning is also known as "combing". This alternate term came about because the practitioner guides their hands over the patient's body in a manner like combing. Direct contact is not applied in this case.

- Imagine your hands removing negative energy, emotions, and toxins.
- Guide your hands like a comb around the patient's head, chest, shoulders, and any other necessary areas. Do this as carefully as possible.
- Imagine the negative energy and toxins falling away and entering the universe (What Are The Reiki Hand Positions And How To Use Them, 2020, para 3).

Tapping:

Cleaning or combing involves a more general approach to healing, while tapping concentrates on a specific area.

- After you have scanned the body, isolate an injured or tense area.
- Place two fingers onto the area.
- Gently tap the area and begin a slow massage.
- Focus on using the universe's energy to unblock the area and remove the tension (What Are The Reiki Hand Positions And How To Use Them, 2020, para 3).

Swiping:

- Swiping restores energy from the left shoulder to the right hip and from the right shoulder to the left hip.
- Begin with your left hand on your right shoulder and, almost like swiping, move your palm diagonally across the body to the right hip.
- Next, start from your left shoulder and move your hand across to your right hip.
- Let the energy from your hands be transferred while you carefully move your hand.
- Repeat this swiping process three times on each side (What Are The Reiki Hand

Positions And How To Use Them, 2020, para 3).

Fast Self-Treatment

If you find that you do not have time to conduct a full cleaning and healing ritual on yourself, Reiki Scoop provides a sample of a fast self-treatment you can use:

- Put your palm on the crown and sacral chakras for three to five minutes.
- Next, place a palm on the third eye and navel chakras.
- Then, move your hands to your throat and solar plexus.
- Finally, position both hands on the heart chakra.

Remember to move down and up the vertical alignment of your chakras. Try to keep the vertical alignment intact so a clear path of energy is created (What Are The Reiki Hand Positions And How To Use Them, 2020, para 4).

~

SEIHEKI CHIRYO HO

If you recall from Okuden, Seiheki Chiryo Ho primarily assists individuals in overcoming negative patterns, namely bad habits and destructive thoughts. Furthermore, it boosts the patient's energy for a clear purpose or target. This is something that can be done alone as part of your self-treatment, or a master can help you with this. Seiheki Chiryo Ho relies on affirmations and repeating mantras to achieve the above.

The website Deborah Reiki provides more insight into the power of Reiki affirmations.

It also provides help with changing mental attitudes (overthinking, planning, controlling, and negative self-talk). Support can be given for stopping smoking, for example. Change happens a step at a time, so the first stage is to decide upon one particular area in your life you want to work on.

The next task is to find an appropriate affirmation. Affirmations need to be both achievable and positive (Working with affirmations: Seiheki Chiryo Ho, 2017).

Self-treatment:

- Name a specific objective you would like to achieve.
- Now specify specific bad habits, patterns

of behavior, or destructive thoughts that prevent you from obtaining the above.
- Repeat personalized affirmations that give you power over the specific bad habit. Here are some examples:

>I will stop smoking.
>I will stop drinking alcohol.
>I will pay attention to the words I say to myself.
>I will exercise more regularly.
>I will use more loving-kind words with myself.

Patient treatment:

- Sit before the patient.
- Listen to the patient as they explain their goals and name the patterns of behavior that create obstructions.
- Remind the patient that it takes time to change patterns of behavior and to implement new habits.
- Indicate to the patient that it all begins with will power. Repeating affirmations is therefore central in helping the individual overcome the negative habit or pattern.
- Encourage the patient to repeat motivating affirmations. Here are some affirmations they can use:

>I will treat myself more kindly.

>I will stop overeating.

>I will say more loving words to myself.

>I will take better care of my body.

>I will not hold on to negative emotions.

When implementing Seiheki Chiryo Ho, remember that it takes time for a new habit to become ingrained. Be patient with yourself during this process of change. Make sure to remind yourself and the patient that movement in a positive and healthy direction is a remarkable thing, but it takes courage, patience, and continuous motivation. Thus, encourage yourself and the patient to consistently repeat these affirmations to inspire motivation.

CONCLUSION

In your Reiki training, you will not be introduced to these techniques all at once. This chapter does not intend for you to master these overnight; rather, its purpose is to summarize Reiki meditation, mastering the hand position steps and techniques, and fitting Seiheki Chiryo Ho into a comprehensive list that you can refer to time and time again long after your Reiki training has ended.

For the next few years and beyond, you can return to a section in this book and concentrate on developing a certain technique. Despite the intention to create a summarized list, a devoted Reiki practitioner will spend their lifetime trying to enhance them. Having said that, the steps and techniques mentioned here can accompany your Shoden, Okuden, and Shinpiden and your life-long Reiki training.

CHAPTER 7
HEALING OTHERS- PART 1

"You are an aperture through which the universe is looking at and exploring itself." –Alan Watts

SELF-HEALING AND REIKI BACKGROUND

The concept of self-healing is layered. First, on a fundamental level, it is misleading as it is not ourselves, but light and energy which heal us; it is the universal energy which heals us. Yet, since we are composed of light and energy, what are we other than the same thing that composes the universe? Also, what are we other than the thing that heals us?

It is circular reasoning at its very best. Yet, that seems to be in line with nature and the universe, which also appear to be circular.

Consider, for example, plants: they create their own food from light and carbon to reproduce themselves. Humans use calories to hunt (or in the present day, work) and, in turn, this gives us more energy. While self-healing may seem like a foreign concept, it happens all the time. When we get sick, our bodies create antibodies to fight off the invaders. We have to do nothing except heal. Unlike our bodies, which first identify the harmful virus or bacteria, we are not aware that we suffer from a spiritual ailment. We do not know that the blockage in our heart chakra is making us unwilling to love or trust people again.

A hundred years ago, Mikao Usui discovered this innate ability of the body to heal itself. It was probably his close encounter with death during the cholera outbreak that assisted Usui in his recovery. "Throughout his education, Dr. Usui had an interest in medicine, psychology, and theology. It was this interest that prompted him to seek a way to heal himself and others using the laying on of hands" (History and Traditions of Reiki, para 2). Therefore, Usui dedicated his education to devise a way of providing self-healing.

～

HEALING FOR THE MIND, BODY, AND SOUL

In preparation for your first attunement and during your 21-day purification, you are encouraged to avoid harmful or poisonous chemicals, bad habits, and holding onto negative emotions. Reiki essentially cleanses the Mind, Body, and Soul. It acknowledges that all are corrupted by physical, emotional, and spiritual toxins (although it is not always the case that if one person is corrupted then the others will be too). This is referred to as the "four alignment" (Brenner, 2016, para 2).

The Physical Alignment

Physical alignment concentrates on anatomy. It concentrates on our material form. Biological processes such as digestion, respiration, reproduction, and others compose part of the physical alignment. Self-healing in Reiki aspires to enhance one's physical processes so that chronic pain is eliminated (Brenner, 2016, para 3).

The Mental Alignment

Elise Brenner succinctly describes the problematic nature of mental misalignment: "The mind is sometimes called the 'organ of misery' because it has the capacity to ruin our days, even our lives, with its incessant rambling and ruminating" (Brenner, 2016, para 3). It is necessary for us to learn how our mind works, then to learn how to purify it. This will prove to be the most challenging, but one which Reiki self-healing can help with through mantras, affirmations, and meditation.

The Emotional Alignment

Emotions can be volatile and unreliable in nature. Sadly, it is not so easy to distance ourselves from them. While we may be encouraged to be more rational and reasonable as opposed to emotional, we should instead strive to be emotionally balanced. As this alignment is separated from the mental alignment, you cannot simply reason with your emotions. Self-healing tackles emotional impurities focusing on the core sources of pain: a lack of emotional energy or the heart or sacral chakra being blocked.

The Spiritual Alignment

While Reiki insists on a balance and alignment of the physical, mental, emotional, and spiritual, if there were one that was most important, it would be spiritual alignment. If we do not experience a direct channel with the universe's energy, we become desolate, lost, and uninspired. We do not realize that we have a "higher being" in us which is capable of immense healing and extraordinary accomplishments. Brenner describes how spiritual alignment is vital:

A state of balance facilitates spiritual growth, allowing the individual to connect to an inner peace and serenity, as well as to a sense of oneness and inter-being with all beings. We experience an openness to life, a sense of spaciousness and expansiveness (2016, para 3).

If you cannot find a balance for your mind, body, and soul, everything will be out of sync. We have already seen that it is primarily imbalance that causes sickness. For example, if you are stressed, you lack the capacity or strength to manage a situation. If you have stiffness in your shoulders, you are not receiving enough blood supply and flow to this area. Reiki uses self-healing to achieve the optimum balance between all these areas.

When saying words such as "alignment" and "integrity", there is intrinsic power that resonates from them. This is like the vibration of symbols. The powerful resonance from words like "integrity" not only demonstrate how holistic the four alignments are, but how intense as well.

∾

SELF-HEALING APPROACHES

Reiki Meditation

Meditation, in fact, is the perfect medium for learning about the mind, which Brenner calls "the organ of misery". When meditating, we have no choice but to contend directly with our brains. There is nothing that can distract us or save us from the mind. It is only through meditation that we can learn how necessary it is to quiet the mind and maintain control over it (Peikon, 2019, para 2).

Reiki meditation not only helps individuals learn how their mind works, but it assists with the four alignments. When you go through the steps of placing a palm on your seven chakras, by vertically moving from one to the next, you are establishing this connection between your mind, body, and soul.

Reiki Bath

You do not need a bathtub for this one. A Reiki bath involves self-cleansing. Like a long soak after a difficult day, the Reiki bath entails a longer Reiki session; it is like a full Reiki treatment. While it is not always practical to give yourself a full treatment, it is advised to do one on yourself once a week or a month.

In the article "How to give yourself a 'reiki bath' for some at-home healing", Fitzmaurice describes how to give yourself a cleansing. The full-treatment begins with choosing a comfortable space, then meditating, going through a chakra alignment process starting with your crown, and repeating the five chakra principles.

Self-Healing With a Master

Finally, if you decide to opt for Reiki training, you can use your sessions with a Reiki master to help you become proficient in self-healing. Learning how to heal yourself is one of the initial aspects of Reiki training. Thus, you will cover this extensively in Shoden. Even if you decide not to do the training, you can visit a master to ask him or her to show you the basics of self-healing. Masters are trained in teaching self-healing, so it is worthwhile to use one of these skilled practitioners for assistance with this.

CHAPTER 8
HEALING OTHERS - PART 2

"Carry out a random act of kindness, with no expectation of reward, safe in the knowledge that one day someone might do the same for you." –Princess Diana

HEALING OTHERS AND REIKI BACKGROUND

When one becomes adept in self-healing, they can then heal another individual and teach that person how to heal themselves. This act is not only about healing; it is also about generational transition: the victim becomes healed, and the victim becomes a healer.

A clear illustration of this is seen in Hawayo Takata. Though she is credited with exporting Reiki to the West and being a proficient healer, unlike other great men, she did not learn this ability innately. After her own close experience with death, she attended Chujiro Hayashi's Reiki clinic, receiving treatment for her bladder disease (Hawayo Takata – The Woman Who Brought Reiki To The Western World, 2020, para 1). Takata is a bright example of how healing through Reiki transitions from one generation to the next. In this sense, Reiki is not simply about healing others, but giving them the tools to heal themselves.

Unfortunately, this is not a vocation for all. Some people do not have the concentration to become a Reiki healer nor do they have the intention. Others will also have other commitments, which are equally important, like the production of food and the provision of electrical power. For this reason, learning to heal others will always be a necessary function of Reiki.

PHYSICAL, PSYCHOLOGICAL, AND EMOTIONAL HEALING FOR OTHERS

It is not always easy to know what ailments individuals suffer from. Since Reiki concentrates on a holistic approach, healing others involves treating various symptoms, all belonging to different dimensions. The

Reiki Association highlights the importance of listening to the patient intently (Code of Ethics of The Reiki Association, 2020) so that you can provide a holistic approach.

Reiki healer Lisa Brandis explains how listening helps her to make informed decisions as a Reiki healer:

When a client first arrives to have a Reiki session with me, I ask them to take a moment to think about why they have come, and [I] ask them to make a note of what they hope to achieve during their Intuitive Reiki session with me (2013, para 1).

On the other hand, patients will not always know the true cause or nature of their ailments. To assist with this, Reiki training emphasizes the importance of aligning with the universal energy, a healer developing their intuition, and mastering Byosen.

Aligning Oneself With Reiki

Before every cleansing or attunement, the Reiki healer needs to invite Reiki into the environment. They also need to state their intention of using Reiki to heal the individual. Brandis discusses the reasoning behind this: "This is a very important step for me as it also allows me to focus and disengage from my own life and really come into a place of openness and receptivity and most importantly love" (Brandis, 2013, para 1).

Before continuing, it should be noted that if you are not familiar with the universe's energy or do not feel skilled enough to harness and transfer that energy, then inform your patient of this before commencing. Generally, it will require a decent amount of time to practice Reiki.

While it is certainly recommended to practice on loved ones and others to master Reiki healing, if you are not confident, you should also inform your patient or loved one. Being honest and building a relationship based on trust is another ethical code you should adhere to as a Reiki practitioner.

When the Reiki healer invites the universe's energy into the environment, they are trying to channel it into the patient. Though the Reiki healer has the universe's energy in them, they are not to be confused with actually *being* the universe's energy. Naturally, it does flow in beings, but the purpose of Reiki sessions is to direct the universe's energy into the patient. To achieve this, the Reiki practitioner needs constant meditation and attunement sessions —either self-attunement sessions or ones with a master.

Developing Intuition

"Intuition is the wisdom from within from our Divine self" (Brandis, 2013, para 2). The universe will always know what remedy to provide to the patient, so healers need to use Reiki to guide them. It is through intuition that the Reiki practitioner can obtain direction and know what healing to offer.

As a Reiki healer, it is your responsibility to be in

touch with the Divine Self. Remember, the "divinity" in you has no prejudice; it does not hate and offers compassion and kindness to all. Thus, before every Reiki session—even with yourself and when practicing on loved ones—you need to meditate and relinquish all prejudice and judgment. As a Reiki healer, it is your responsibility to reach a higher state that is free from all kinds of judgment. Meditation and attending many attunements can assist in strengthening this bond with the higher self.

In Shinpiden, you cover Holy Fire ignition, which is the process of separating oneself from their ego. You may have not reached Usui Reiki Level III, but it is recommended when practicing on patients that you learn to distance yourself from your ego. Once the ego has no grasp over you, you can discover your divine, or true, self.

Once you have obtained this connection with your divine self, then you can focus on your intuition's guidance of the patient's treatment. When performing a scan or Byosen, pay attention to anything that does not seem right. If you sense something is off, do not rationalize but rather use your intuition to provide the necessary healing.

We analyzed this earlier, but if an area is too hot or too cold, do not assume there is no issue. An assumption is generally filtered information. The initial signal is the heat or lack of pulse in the area.

DISTANCE HEALING

In Okuden, you learned about five different symbols, one of which was Hon Sha Ze Sho Nen. Hon Sha Ze Sho Nen, meaning "no past, no present, no future", reveals that healing does not have any spatial or temporal boundaries (Price, 2019). Thus, it is possible to heal people through online platforms. Meditating and visualizing this symbol will help you to access and harness this kind of healing.

In Portland Helmich's article, the Reiki healer, Libby Barnett, claims that she has moved her Reiki treatment to an online platform (Helmich, 2020). The International Center for Reiki Training seems to verify that distance healing is a new direction for Reiki. (Lipinski).

When offering the Reiki healing, remember to include the Hon Sha Ze Sho Nen symbol in your treatment and cleansing so that you can incorporate this healing over a distance.

HEALING LOVED ONES

Many medical professionals are forbidden from treating their loved ones. Psychologists and doctors must follow these regulations (Treating Self or Family, 2020). Reiki healers do not have the same kinds of regulations (Code of Ethics of the Reiki Association, 2020). This gives you the opportunity to practice on friends, family members, and even pets.

There are two principal reasons for this. First, you

as a Reiki healer or master are a channel through which the universe acts. In your quest as a practitioner, your aim is to distance yourself as much as possible from your ego. This separation from the ego allows the universe to act through you. Secondly, Reiki is generally safe (Saleh, 2020, para 6). Nevertheless, as a practitioner, you should do all that you can to carry out Reiki in a safe environment. You should also take your commitment to the patient's well-being seriously, even if they are your friend or pet.

Therefore, when offering to heal a family member, be earnest about their treatment; this will help you to advance as a Reiki healer. Furthermore, similar to providing healing to others, if your loved one feels uncomfortable or reluctant, then do not persist with the treatment as they are averse to that specific cleaning or attunement ritual, or stop with the treatment altogether if they wish it so.

CONCLUSION

While it is genuinely exciting to wish to heal others, it is not easy. Being a Reiki healer is hard work; helping people with their emotional, psychological, physical, and spiritual ailments is not straightforward. This vocation demands separation from the ego, relinquishing all judgment and prejudice, a commitment to self-growth, and the humblest intention of healing others. This is the reason why not everyone is a Reiki master. In the past, "traditionally, the Reiki master level of training was by invitation only" (Can I Learn

Reiki Myself?, 2016, para 4). Being a Reiki master and healer is a big responsibility.

If you decide to continue with your Reiki healer, it is vital to acknowledge all the hours you need to spend studying the theory and applying the practices. Besides these duties, it is also important to remember that you need to relinquish your pride and be committed to the emotional, physical, spiritual, and psychological well-being of others.

CHAPTER 9

FAQ

In this chapter, we will spend time answering some questions beginners generally propose when learning about Reiki. We hope to clarify any doubts and concerns regarding Reiki in the process. While this section aims to provide as much information as possible, it cannot be as exhaustive as we would like. In this case, it will deal with the most pressing and common questions and concerns in order to provide readers with a little bit more understanding.

- **How much do Reiki sessions cost, and how many sessions do I need?**

First, people typically do not attend one Reiki session. As the 21-day detox indicates, it takes a long time for toxins of all forms to leave your body. Attending one Reiki session might provide immediate relief, but long-term, it is advisable to attend regular Reiki sessions.

One session is usually priced between $60 and $90 (K., n.d.). However, there are many prospective Reiki healers who intend to strengthen their abilities and will charge you less. Try visiting a local Reiki institute and asking them if any students—typically Reiki Level II—healers wish to cement their Reiki practice.

The number of Reiki sessions can vary. Sometimes, patients only seek assistance with a minor ailment and will need just one session, while other patients might wish to find therapy for the mind, body, and soul, necessitating regular sessions with a practitioner (Bedosky, 2020, p. para 9).

- **How much is a Reiki course, and how long are the programs?**

Reiki courses vary in price and length. There are numerous online courses available on Udemy offering Reiki training in Levels I and II over two days. While it is certainly possible, if you are interested in becoming more proficient at Reiki, attending a course that spans six months is probably best.

Keep in mind that the longer the course is, the more expensive it will be. An online course from Udemy is about $130. However, online courses from websites such as Reiki Infinite Healer are priced from as little as $49. If you feel more comfortable training in person, the courses will cost a bit more. In-center, Reiki Level I and II courses start from $300. While it is not always so practical, in-center classes are strongly recommended as they spend a lot of time applying Reiki practices.

Online and in-center courses offer intensive programs that can be completed in two days. Though, when you are finished, you will need to do the 21-day purification process. That means that after Reiki Level II, you can only finish Reiki Level I and II training in about a month. However, more thorough organizations require a 21-day purification after Reiki Level I, adding another month to the training.

- **Is there a Reiki community that can support me during my training?**

If you attend an in-center Reiki course, you will be part of a group. Generally, Reiki training programs require group participation to allow the prospective healers the opportunity to practice on others. As a result, when you begin your training, you are introduced to a group of trainees, and you grow in Reiki together.

This is the same for online training. You do not train alone. While it may be more isolated to train online, you can always join an online forum afterward. You could also go to your local Reiki center and ask about a Reiki community near you.

It is suggested that you try to find a local Reiki clinic. Often, they need healers and trainees, so you can offer your services and further your development in the practice.

• Where do I find a Reiki healer or master?

As Reiki has become popular in recent years, clinics devoted to the practice are opening up in various cities worldwide. Try searching for a local clinic for a Reiki healer or master.

Additionally, as with many things these days, Reiki has gone digital. You can also try booking a session with an online Reiki healer. While this is more practical, it is always best during your first few sessions to be in the physical presence of a healer.

• How long is a Reiki session?

Reiki sessions are one hour, though there are some that last an hour and a half (Reiki Sessions – What To Expect, 2020). You need to arrive 15 minutes before your Reiki session so that your healer can explain what you can expect from your session.

• Is there a code of ethics for Reiki?

Yes. The Reiki Association consistently updates its code of ethics for Reiki healers. It is necessary for

Reiki practitioners to remain informed of new regulations. This is one of the ethics of a Reiki practitioner.

You can visit the Reiki Association's site to learn this code of ethics to help you be compliant should you wish to be a Reiki healer (Code of Ethics of the Reiki Association, 2020).

- **How do I prepare for a Reiki session?**

You will be lying on a Reiki stretcher or bed while the healer performs the cleansing, so make sure the clothes that you are in are comfortable. Before your first session, try to also be 15 minutes early as the practitioner will discuss your treatment with you prior to the cleansing (Reiki Sessions – What To Expect, 2020).

If you feel uncomfortable with anything that the Reiki healer explains about your upcoming treatment, mention it to him or her before commencing.

- **Does Reiki really work?**

Many studies conducted have shown positive results suggesting that Reiki is a holistic therapy. While research has extensively shown the effectiveness of Reiki healing, scientists have still not discovered how Reiki works.

In the future, it is possible that scientists will be able to solve this mystery. However, for now, as it remains, Reiki has been proven to help many recover from physical ailments, chronic pain, and mental health issues (Lotus, 2011) (Kisner, 2020) (Newman, 2017).

- **Do I need to attend a Reiki course?**

No, you do not need to attend a Reiki course. If you would like to receive healing for physical discomfort, stress, burnout, regulating your emotions, or increasing your motivation, you can attend Reiki sessions with a healer.

Alternatively, you might find Reiki Level I useful in teaching you about self-healing. Reiki Level II focuses on healing others, so attending Reiki Level I could help you to integrate Reiki practices into your lifestyle. In this case, it is still recommended to see a healer for they will transfer Reiki to you so that you can begin healing on all dimensions.

- **What should I expect from my first Reiki session?**

There is no single answer for this as everyone experiences something different. Some people may become extremely sensitive since toxins have been removed from their bodies, while others may feel lighter and more joyous. After your first Reiki session, it is important to drink a lot of liquids because it can be rather strenuous.

Think of Reiki as a spiritual massage. During your first session, you will remain fully clothed and will lie down on a stretcher or bed. The healer will use various hand positions to channel the universe's energy into your seven chakras, as well as into any other areas experiencing discomfort, such as your shoulders. The healer will explain everything that will happen in the Reiki session before commencing so you will kn0w what to expect.

- **What are the best resources to practice Reiki?**

Reiki has become digital, so you can make use of extensive online tools like podcasts, articles, YouTube videos, and blogs. There are also various institutes and academies providing Reiki training and work-shops. However, the best Reiki guidance and mastery can come from Reiki masters themselves. While it may seem daunting to have private lessons with a Reiki master, it is really the most ideal thing you can do.

Furthermore, there are many books written by Reiki healers. Some of these books include Amy Z. Rowland's *The Complete Book of Traditional Reiki*, Bodo J. Baginski and Shalila Sharamon's *Reiki Universal Life Energy*, and Phylameana Lila Desy's *Everything Guide to Reiki*.

Training in person at a Reiki center will also put you in contact with people who can guide you on your Reiki journey and show you the most efficient way to develop your practices.

- **Is Reiki affiliated with any religion, and do I have to join a religion to practice Reiki?**

Many modern individuals are beginning to see Buddhism as a way of life rather than a religion. In this sense, Buddhist philosophy provides moral codes and principles that help one live a more meaningful and happier life. Since Reiki originates from Tendai, Qigong, and Mahayana varieties of Buddhism, the Buddhist way of life and codes certainly influence Reiki.

Nonetheless, the codes and morals Reiki derives from Buddhism do not dictate religious principles nor require practitioners to maintain religious beliefs. With that said, Reiki is a spiritual experience. It aims to provide patients, students, teachers, and healers with a link to their higher self. This is not intrinsically rooted in religious notions, but it does essentially focus on a spiritual experience. Some atheists and secularists do not believe in a soul, so they will find it difficult to accept this Reiki principle and practice.

CHAPTER 10
OTHER BOOKS BY EMILY ODDO

Here's a list of Emily Oddo books you can find on Amazon:

Yoga for Beginners:

Chakras for Beginners:

Reiki For Beginners:

Third Eye:

AFTERWORD

REIKI HEALERS IN HISTORY

In the West, we are raised on tales of Jesus using touch to heal the lives of those afflicted with physical ailments, such as blindness. In the East, people are brought up on Buddhist, Shinto, and Taoist philosophies, repeating how Buddha was able to heal those from their physical illnesses.

Two thousand years later, we still know of these great healers and their remarkable feats. While Jesus and Buddha provided their followers and those who met them with much spiritual guidance and relief from physical agony, they also blessed the world with the knowledge that physical touch can be a source of remedy and revival.

However, as their stories pass from generation to generation, we call their feats miracles, and the capability of offering healing through physical touch becomes more and more questionable, and ultimately, unobtainable. It is believed to be a miracle that can only be performed by spiritual leaders or great men. This is when the religions have a monopoly over this practice and we as humans forget our own capacities to perform these very acts.

Reiki has not allowed us to forget. A hundred years ago, when he had a close encounter with death, Mikao Usui realized it is important that we do not forget that our bodies are made of light and energy. And if we are essentially light and energy, then all we need is light and energy and a channel to these two sources to heal. Always remember the wisdom the great healers of our past have blessed us with.

ANCIENT MEDICINE AND MODERN NECESSITY

Unfortunately, we have quite forgotten our close connection to energy and light. Though religions have not always served us well, belief systems such as Hinduism, Buddhism, Taoism, and even Christianity reminded us how necessary it was to be spiritually healthy and to rid the body of toxins.

For example, Lent in the Christian faith aims to remove an individual's harmful habit for 40 days; it is comparable to the two 21-day detoxes performed after the Shoden and Okuden attunements. These belief systems not only placed an emphasis on spiritual cleanliness but on compassion and kindness to others, as well as emotional and psychological well-being, which lives in our minds yet transcends our physical forms to be of immense utility to others.

In years long past, people turned to ancient medicine as a necessity. Both Mikao Usui and Hawayo Takata had close encounters with death that led them to Reiki. It was their desperation for survival that drew them to the practice. Once healed with it, Takata went on to live until the age of eighty (Bennet, p 4). During her long life, she opened Reiki clinics in the US and spread the power of energy and light healing far and wide.

We have made so much progress in regards to increasing the human lifespan, but we have forgotten that energy and light are essential components to our healing. Not all of us have forgotten, though. For example, light therapy is a New Age treatment that can help lessen the impact of seasonal depression. Yet, despite our progress, people are still sick, continuing to consume harmful chemicals and hold onto anger, draining them of their vitality.

People still lead lives where the consumption of harmful toxins is common practice. People ingest copious amounts of sugar, flooding their bodies with artificial but sought-after energy. It is the same with alcohol; even though it slowly and excruciatingly dehydrates their systems, it provides them with the willingness to party late into the night. The next day is another story, though, as their bodies are completely deprived of all nutrients, electrolytes, and energy. It is a high price to pay.

The currency is energy, and it is the only currency

we innately need and are now seeking through artificial but unwholesome sources. Our bodies crave
sugar because we desire vitality. Remember, though,
that on a purely molecular level, we are energy and
light. Our cells are nuclei and mitochondria, and our
atoms, protons, and electrons.

Somehow, we think that by supplying our bodies
with artificial and unsustainable forms of energy like
sugar and caffeine, we will be able to replace pure
substances such as light and energy. Yes, go on and
try to feed a plant some sugar. Surely, if you gave a
plant caffeine, it would grow better and more
quickly. I am being sarcastic now, but we have to
consider biology deeply. Plants need light just like us,
and they also need energy just like us.

The currency is always energy. Redbull, Star-
bucks, and Nestle all know that deep down, you
need a boost. But the more you rely on anything but
light and energy to restore your vitality, the more
these companies have you chained like a dog.

Our crisis in energy is indicated clearly in the rise
in stress, burnout, anxiety, and depression. It is not
that life has become too much to handle, but that we
are deprived of the necessary stamina to handle it.
The sad truth is that the more intense the burnout
and stress gets, the more we believe we are weak and
destined for sickness.

We have forgotten that our ancestors like Usui
and Takata once turned to the universe's energy for
their lives. If they could do it a hundred years ago,
we can surely do it now, and if Jesus and Buddha

used the universe's energy as a remedy for physical ailments and spiritual desolation two thousand years ago, we can definitely do it now.

REIKI AS AN ETERNAL SOURCE OF HEALING

Reiki is an instinctual language that we communicate to provide comfort to others. Consider a hug when you really need comforting. Why do you feel like you need a hug sometimes? The emphasis is on the word "need". Remind yourself of the time you last needed a good embrace. Perhaps you heard really bad news and needed the comfort words could not offer. And when you received that hug, maybe it brought you to tears. It opened a channel in your heart that you didn't know existed. Your sensitivity was frightening at that moment, and so you swallowed your tenderness and spent the next few days or years trying not to look at that sensitivity again.

Yet, that sensitivity was a clue. It showed you an area of tenderness that needed your attention. A hug helped because physical touch can heal that. The problem is that after the hug, you neglected that sensitivity and did not seek a channel to provide it with the necessary healing.

Reiki is that channel. The ancient wisdom of Reiki revived by Usui recognizes how our chakras are tender openings. The essence of spiritual vitality is directed through the chakras, giving us healing to the various dimensions of our being: spiritual, psychological, emotional, and physical. Unblocking one chakra generally entails healing an individual in every dimension.

Consider the heart chakra, Anahata; channeling energy to it through a hand position or drawing Shika Sei Ki over the region can soothe palpitations and decrease chest pain. Meditating and reflecting on Shika Sei Ki or contemplating the power of Anahata can soothe loneliness and prepare an individual to love again after a negative romantic encounter.

Reiki for Beginners serves to be a guide to help newcomers incorporate Reiki practices into their everyday lives and into those of their loved ones. Since Reiki has formally been established for more roughly a century, much has been researched and written about it. Furthermore, it has entered the domain of the internet, where information is limitless.

This guide serves not to be an exhaustive discussion on Reiki, nor does it aim to cover all the various Reiki techniques, but it does intend to go over the main concepts and healing approaches, namely attunements, hand positions, spiritual detox, and meditation.

Many Reiki websites and institutions are constantly updating their knowledge. *Reiki for Beginners* intends to complement them. As Reiki is a necessary practice for personal and communal healing, the utility and benefits of the practice should always be underlined and extended to all. However, this guide aims most of all to inform its readers as to why they should choose Reiki as an alternative and holistic healing approach. It aims to explain the practical value of Reiki while outlining how physical touch, meditation, spiritual cleanliness, and attunement to divinity are not confined to Reiki healing, but rather highlighted by Reiki.

Healing Hands

Our language does provide us with clues on the power of physical touch. We often refer to "healing hands of love" or the "healing hands of God". Oftentimes, God is represented simply as hands while other religious figures such as Jesus are displayed with an emphasis on his hands. What we have inherited is a tradition that acknowledges how significant hands are. The clue is in the phrase "healing hands". It is ancient wisdom that we derive from the days of Buddha, Jesus, and the reign of the Roman Catholic Church during the days of the Western Roman Empire.

The problem is it is not a mainstream medical treatment. Though many medical breakthroughs have been achieved through science, we often enter the pharmaceutical trap, finding relief from one ailment while being burdened with the next. It is not a mainstream alternative yet, but it is a reliable healing system we have used since the dawn of man.

When we have stomach aches or suffer from nausea, to provide relief, we rub our bellies, or even better, get a loved one to do so. When we suspect an injury may be a broken bone, we check the area to see if our suspicions are confirmed. When we or someone we love feels vulnerable, we put our arms around ourselves or our loved ones to form a circle of protection. When we feel a great spasm of pain in our arms, legs, feet, or hands, our immediate reaction is to clutch on to the area. Once the pain subsides, we rub the area to heal it, subconsciously letting blood flow to it. Lastly, if someone cannot sleep, we caress or massage them. If it is a newborn baby, we rock it gently to help with the restlessness.

Healing through hands has become codified in our nature. Like other mammals, we rely on physical touch to care for our young, protect our loved ones, and heal ourselves. We will not lose this ability because it is innate; it is something given to us by the universe in our genes.

We should welcome medical breakthroughs, because one day, they will incorporate physical touch more extensively in their programs. There are already physiotherapists, masseuses, and chiropractors who are in the medical world providing healing to others through "healing hands".

Reiki Responsibility

On a final note, Reiki masters, healers, and practitioners have much responsibility. Firstly, they are working with an intimate space of people who are from walks of life. As Reiki has been exported to the West, it also has to embrace but work with the diversity of Western societies. Some people may be comfortable with attunements, hand positions, and meditations, but not all people will be. As you are in such close physical proximity, you should be mindful of this and open to a variety of patients. Furthermore, you should always do your best to communicate openly with your patients so that they know what to expect.

Secondly, you are not only dealing with patients on a physical but also on spiritual, psychological, and emotional levels. This is a large burden to carry as individuals suffer from a range of psychological and emotional problems. This includes things like trauma, abuse, nihilism, or a lack of self-esteem. To be part of the process that encourages positive change in people's lives is not easy. That being said, it is immensely rewarding.

As a prospective Reiki healer, you are enriching the lives of others on every level. The responsibility of this duty should not be understated. People need healing in times of spiritual crisis. Reiki is one of the few modern-day approaches that provide holistic healing.

Good luck on your Reiki journey!

REFERENCES

420 Naval Ravikant Quotes to Make You Happy [and Wealthy]. (n.d.). *Wisdom Quotes*. https://wisdomquotes.com/naval-ravikant-quotes/

5 Signs That A Reiki Cleanse Would Benefit You. (2019, June 3). *Crystal Palace Osteopaths & Natural Therapies*. https://www.crystalpalaceosteopaths.co.uk/5-signs-that-a-reiki-cleanse-would-benefit-you/

Achanta, R. (2017, September 28). Reiki Meditation – How To Do And What Are Its Benefits? *Style Craze*. https://www.stylecraze.com/articles/simple-steps-to-practice-reiki-meditation/

Ankh - Egyptian Symbol of Life. (2015, November 5). *NPS*. https://www.nps.gov/afbg/learn/historyculture/ankh.htm

Beaming. (2018). *Rae Jae*. http://raejae.com/reiki/learn-more/what-is-beaming

Bedosky, L. (2020, May 13). Reiki for Beginners FAQs: Everything You Need to Know to Get Started.

Everyday   Health.   https://www.everydayhealth.-com/reiki/beginners-faqs-everything-you-need-to-know-to-get-started/

Bennet, A. (n.d.). Reiki: Accessing the Human Energetic System. *Mountain   Quest   Institute.* https://www.academia.edu/17435888/REIKI_Accessing_the_Human_Energetic_System?auto=download&email_work_card=download-paper

Brandis, L. (2013, May 18). Intuitive Reiki. *International Institute for Complementary Therapies.* https://www.iict.co.uk/articles/15-featured-member/1445-intuitive-reiki

Brenner, E. (2016, August 30). Reiki: A Gateway to Healing Mind, Body and Soul. *Natural Awakenings Boston.*   https://www.naturalawakeningsboston.-com/2016/08/30/251357/reiki-a-gateway-to-healing-mind-body-and-soul

Burgess, L. (2018, November 23). Foot massage techniques and benefits. *Medical News Today.* https://www.medicalnewstoday.com/articles/323790

Can I Learn Reiki Myself? (2016). *Taking Charge of Your Wellbeing. https://www.takingcharge.csh.umn.edu/can-i-learn-reiki-myself*

Classes. (n.d.). *Reiki by Nataki.* http://www.reikibynataki.com/reiki-magnified-healing-classes.html

Code of Ethics of The Reiki Association. (2020). *Association, The Reiki.* https://www.reikiassociation.net/code-of-ethics.php

Cross. (2020). Britannica. https://www.britannica.com/topic/cross-religious-symbol

Dai Ko Myo Reiki Master Symbol And Reiki

Level   3   Shinpiden.   (2020).   *Reiki   Scoop.*
https://reikiscoop.com/dai-ko-myo-reiki-master-
symbol-and-reiki-level-3-shinpiden/

DiGiulio, S. (2018, August 2). How to spot (and
deal   with)   an   energy   vampire.   *NBCnews.*
https://www.nbcnews.com/better/health/how-
spot-deal-energy-vampire-ncna896251

Elflein, J. (2016, August 16). Stress and burnout -
Statistics & Facts. *Statista.* https://www.statista.-
com/topics/2099/stress-and-burnout/

Exploring Mikao Usui's Teachings. (2014, May
25). *The International House of Reiki.* https://ihreiki.-
com/blog/exploring_mikao_usuis_teachings/?
v=68caa8201064.

Fleming, D. (2018, February 14). Get Your Life
Moving in the Right Direction with Reiki. *Reiki Rays.*
https://reikirays.com/40783/life-moving-right-
direction-reiki/

Giaser. (2020, May 13). Beaming Reiki Technique.
Holy Reiki Fire. https://www.holyfirereiki.eu/beam-
ing-reiki-technique/

Hawayo Takata – The Woman Who Brought Reiki
To   The   Western   World.   (2020).   *Reiki   Scoop.*
https://reikiscoop.com/hawayo-takata-the-woman-
who-brought-reiki-to-the-western-world/

Healthwise Staff. (2019, June 26). Knee Problems
and   Injuries.   *UOFM   Health.*
https://www.uofmhealth.org/health-library/kneep

Helmich, P. (2020). Sending Healing Energy
Across Space and Time: The Practice of Long-
Distance   Reiki.   *Kripalu.*   https://kripalu.org/re-

sources/sending-healing-energy-across-space-and-time-practice-long-distance-reiki

History and Traditions of Reiki. (n.d.). *IARP.* https://iarp.org/history-of-reiki/

How Meditation and Reiki can help you stop smoking. (2020). *Reiki-Meditation.co.uk.* https://www.reiki-meditation.co.uk/how-meditation-and-reiki-can-help-you-stop-smoking/

How to Tell, Buddist or Taoist or Confucian Qigong? (2017, December 29). *One Energy.* shorturl.at/cwRV9

Hubris. (2020, December 11). *Wikipedia.* https://en.wikipedia.org/wiki/Hubris

Insomnia Statistics. (2018, December 10). *The Good Body.* https://www.thegoodbody.com/insomnia-statistics/

K., J. (n.d.). How much does a reiki session cost? *Thervo.* https://thervo.com/costs/reiki-session-cost

King, M. L. (1963). *Strength to Love.* New York City: Harper & Row.

Kisner, J. (2020, April). Reiki Can't Possibly Work. So Why Does It? The Atlantic. https://www.theatlantic.com/magazine/archive/2020/04/reiki-cant-possibly-work-so-why-does-it/606808/

Learning Reiki. (n.d.). *The International Centre for Reiki Training.* https://www.reiki.org/faqs/learning-reiki

Lipinski, K. (n.d.). Distant Healing and the Human Energy Field. *The International Training Centre.* https://www.reiki.org/articles/distant-healing-and-human-energy-field

Lottery winners who blew the lot. (2020, April 02). *Lovemoney.* https://www.lovemoney.com/gallerylist/64958/lottery-winners-who-blew-the-lot

Lotus, G. (2011). Reiki Really Works: A Groundbreaking Scientific Study. *UCLAhealth.* https://www.uclahealth.org/rehab/workfiles/urban%20zen/research%20articles/reiki_really_works-a_groundbreaking_scientific_study.pdf

Mitochondria. (2014). *Nature.com.* https://www.nature.com/scitable/topicpage/mitochondria-14053590/

More Concerning Reiju. (2005). *James Deacon's Reiki Pages.* https://www.aetw.org/reiki_reiju2.htm

Newman, T. (2017, 6 September). Everything you need to know about reiki. *Medical News Today.* https://www.medicalnewstoday.com/articles/308772

Peikon, M. (2019). How Nature Awakens a Meditative State. *Wanderlust.* https://wanderlust.com/journal/how-nature-awakens-a-meditative-state/

Petter, F. A. (n.d.). Understanding Byosen Scanning, Part II. *The International Centre for Reiki Training.* https://wanderlust.com/journal/how-nature-awakens-a-meditative-state/

Price, N. J. (2019, September 29). Universal Symbols: The Calming Sei Hei Ki. *Kindred Spirit.* https://kindredspirit.co.uk/2019/09/29/universal-symbols-the-calming-sei-he-ki/

Price, N. J. (2019, October 13). Universal Symbols: The Distant Healing Hon Sha Ze Sho Nen. *Kindred*

Spirit. https://kindredspirit.co.uk/2019/10/13/universal-symbols-the-distant-healing-hon-sha-ze-sho-nen/

Price, N. J. (September, 19 2019). Universal Symbols: The Power of the Cho Ku Rei. *Kindred Spirit.* https://kindredspirit.co.uk/2019/09/15/universal-symbols-the-power-of-the-cho-ku-rei/

Punjabi, P. (2015, November 29). Reiki Symbols Revealed: Shika So and Shika Sei Ki. *Reiki Rays.* https://reikirays.com/28047/reiki-symbols-shika-so-shika-sei-ki/

Qigong. (2020, December 01). *Wikipedia.* https://en.wikipedia.org/wiki/Qigong

Quest, P. (2003). The Attunement Experience. *The International Centre for Reiki Training.* https://www.reiki.org/articles/attunement-experience .

Reiju and Attunements. (n.d.). *International House of Reiki.* https://ihreiki.com/reiki_info/five_elements_of_reiki/reiju_and_attunements/?v=68caa8201064

Reiki 1 Attunement Process. (2020). *Reiki Store.* https://reiki-store.com/

Reiki. (2019). *Encyclopedia.com.* https://www.encyclopedia.com/medicine/divisions-diagnostics-and-procedures/medicine/reiki

Reiki Attunement - The Process and Purpose. (n.d.). *Centre of Excellence.* https://www.centreofexcellence.com/reiki-attunement-process-purpose/

Reiki Hand Positions. (2014, February 24). *The*

Thirsty Soul. *https://thethirstysoul.com/tag/reiki-hand-positions/*

Reiki Level 2 | OKUDEN – What To Expect From It And Its Symbols. (2020). *Reiki Scoop.* https://reikiscoop.com/reiki-level-2-okuden-what-to-expect-from-it-and-its-symbols/.

Reiki Master Attunement. (n.d.). *Balance on Buffalo.* https://balanceonbuffalo.com/reiki/reiki-master-attunement.

Reiki Master Attunement. (n.d.). *International Spiritual Experience.* http://www.internationalspiritual-experience.com/reiki-mikao-usui/reiki-attunements/reiki-level-master-attunement

Reiki popularity growing. (2015, July 17). *ABC Action News.* https://www.youtube.com/watch?v=JU9Au7ILRh4

Reiki Self-Treatment: Procedure Details. (2019, March 20). *Cleveland Clinic.* https://my.clevelandclinic.org/health/treatments/21080-reiki-self-treatment/procedure-details

Reiki Sessions – What To Expect. (2020). *IARP.* https://iarp.org/reiki-sessions-what-to-expect/

Sahasrāra Chakra. (2019). *Chakras.* https://www.chakras.net/energy-centers/sahasrara/about-the-sahasrara-chakra

Saleh, N. (2020, July 30). What Is Reiki? *Very Well Mind.* https://www.verywellmind.com/is-reiki-for-real-1123851

Salguero, C. P. (2016). Paging Dr. Dharma. *Tricycle.* https://tricycle.org/magazine/paging-dr-dharma/

Seiheki Chiryo Ho. (2006, August 29). James

Deacon's Reiki Pages. http://www.aetw.org/d_sei-heiki.html

Snyder, S. (2017, October 2). Chakra Tune-Up: Intro to the Manipura. *Yoga Journal.* https://www.yogajournal.com/yoga-101/intro-navel-chakra-manipura

Stiene, F. (2012, August 17). The Confusion around Reiju. *The International House of Reiki.* https://ihreiki.com/blog/the_confusion_around_reiju/?v=68caa8201064

Suicide Statistics. (2020, March 20). *Befrienders Worldwide.* https://www.befrienders.org/suicide-statistics

Synder, S. (2017, April 13). Chakra Tune-Up: Intro to the Svadhisthana. *Yoga Journal.* https://www.yogajournal.com/yoga-101/intro-sacral-chakra-svadhisthana

The History of Reiki 1865 - 1926. (2011). *Practical Reiki.* https://www.practicalreiki.com/history-of-reiki.html

The Power of Symbols. (2017, May 01). *Innovative Resources.* https://innovativeresources.org/the-power-of-symbols/

The School of Life: An Interview With Alain de Botton. (2019). *The Daily Stoic.* https://dailystoic.com/alain-de-botton/

Third Eye Chakra - Ajna. (n.d.). *Chakras Anatomy.* https://www.chakra-anatomy.com/third-eye-chakra.html

Treating Self or Family. (2020). AMA Association. https://journalofethics.ama-assn.org/article/ama-code-medical-ethics-opinion-physicians-treating-family-members/2012-05

Vishuddha Chakra: The Throat Center. (2020). *The Yoga Sanctuary.* https://www.theyogasanctuary.biz/vishuddha-chakra/

What Are The Reiki Hand Positions And How To Use Them. (2020). *Reiki Scoop.* https://reikiscoop.com/what-are-the-reiki-hand-positions-and-how-to-use-them/

What Is A Reiki Attunement And Why Is It Necessary To Get One. (2020). *Reiki Scoop.* https://reikiscoop.com/what-is-a-reiki-attunement-and-why-is-it-necessary-to-get-one/

What is Holy Fire Reiki? (2019). *Reiki Maya.* *https://reikimaya.com/what-is-holy-fire-reiki-2/*

What to Expect During and After a Reiki Attunement. (2020). *Clear Heart Healing Arts.* http://www.clearhearthealingarts.com/what-to-expect/

Who Is Mikao Usui And The 3 Things You Have To Know About Him. (2020). *Reiki Scoop.* https://reikiscoop.com/who-is-mikao-usui-and-the-3-things-you-have-to-know-about-him/

Working with affirmations: Seiheki Chiryo Ho. (2017, August 29). *Deborah Reiki.* https://deborahreiki.com/2017/08/29/working-with-affirmations-seiheki-chiryo-ho/

IMAGE REFERENCES

(2017). Hand Mom Hold Power Energy (Pixabay) [Photo]. https://pixabay.com/photos/hand-mom-hold-power-energy-2634753/

Altmann, G (2017) Galaxy Space Universe Astronautics (Pixabay) [Photo]. Freiburg, Germany. https://pixabay.com/illustrations/galaxy-space-universe-astronautics-2643089/

Altmann, G (2018) Beyond Death Faith Sky God (Pixabay) [Photo]. Freiburg, Germany. https://pixabay.com/illustrations/galaxy-space-universe-astronautics-2643089/

Chanel, A (2017). Human People Images & Pictures (Unsplash) [Photo]. Boynton Beach, USA. https://unsplash.com/photos/RJCslxmvBcs

Ferreria, M. Dai Ko Myo (Pinterest) [Photo]. https://za.pinterest.com/pin/457467274652963485/

Goldman, M. Instructional pictures demonstrating hand placements for conducting a basic Reiki self treatment. (Pinterest) [Photo]. https://za. pinterest.com/pin/497155246359434893/

Goldman, M. Instructional pictures demonstrating hand placements for conducting a basic Reiki self treatment. (Pinterest) [Photo]. https://za. pinterest.com/pin/497155246359434919/

Goldman, M. Instructional pictures demonstrating hand placements for conducting a basic Reiki self treatment. (Pinterest) [Photo]. https://za. pinterest.com/pin/497155246359434901/.

Hurst, B. Chakra Oils Seven Chakras Set. (Pinterest) [Photo]. https://za.pinterest. com/pin/985231158415577/.

Halacious (2017). A ball of energy with electricity beaming all over the place. [Photo]. https:// unsplash.com/photos/OgvqXGL7XO4.

Irina L (2018). Woman Relaxation Portrait. (Pixabay) [Photo]. Los Angeles, USA. https://pixabay. com/photos/woman-relaxation-portrait-3053492/.

Pilney, C (2014). Reiki Symbols (Pinterest) [Photo]. https://za.pinterest.com/pin/684336105858801126/.

Ramiah, B. Twelve Hand Positions Used for Conducting a Reiki Session: Crown and Top of the Head (Pinterest) [Photo]. https://za.pinterest. com/pin/554013191638825263/.

Ramiah, B. How to Position Your Hands for Self-Healing with Reiki: Neck Collarbone and Heart (Pinterest) [Photo].

shorturl.at/mqCN8

Rübig, J (2013). Wellness Massage Reiki. (Pixabay)

[Photo]. Haßfurt, Germany. https://pixabay.com/ photos/wellness-massage-reiki-285590/.

ScienceFreak (2020). Chakras (Pixabay) [Photo]. Germany. https://unsplash.com/photos/A87rz-MJN_E .

SecondFromTheSun0 (2015). Massage Healing Woman Treatment. [Photo]. https://pixabay.com/ photos/massage-healing-woman-treatment-835468/ .

Socha, A (2020). Buddha Statue Thailand Buddhism (Pixabay) [Photo]. Stockholm, Sweden. https://pixabay.com/photos/buddha-statue-thailand-buddhism-5410319/ .

Street, J (2019). Buddha. [Photo]. https:// unsplash.com/photos/88IMbX3wZmI .

Wahid, A (2018). Taktsang Monastery (Unsplash) [Photo]. Taktsang, Bhutan. https://unsplash.com/ photos/A87rz-MJN_E .

26427586R00094